CW00747539

WHAT A JOURNEY

WHAT A JOURNEY

Autobiography of Rev. Leo Kuykendall

WRITTEN BY

LEO KUYKENDALL

XULON PRESS

Xulon Press
2301 Lucien Way #415
Maitland, FL 32751
407.339.4217
www.xulonpress.com

© 2022 by Leo Kuykendall

All rights reserved solely by the author. The author guarantees all contents are original and do not infringe upon the legal rights of any other person or work. No part of this book may be reproduced in any form without the permission of the author.

Due to the changing nature of the Internet, if there are any web addresses, links, or URLs included in this manuscript, these may have been altered and may no longer be accessible. The views and opinions shared in this book belong solely to the author and do not necessarily reflect those of the publisher. The publisher therefore disclaims responsibility for the views or opinions expressed within the work.

Unless otherwise indicated, Scripture quotations taken from the King James Version (KJV) – *public domain.*

Paperback ISBN-13: 978-1-66286-097-3
Hard Cover ISBN-13: 978-1-66286-098-0
Ebook ISBN-13: 978-1-66286-099-7

How Is Your Reading? Is It:

1. Thoughtless reading;
2. Surface reading;
3. Intense reading;
4. Absorbing reading
5. Informing reading?

READ FOR

Joy
Information
Instruction
Knowledge
Inspiration

Preface

As you get older, there is a tendency to forget names. They are the easiest things to forget. So, I sat down and began to write down the teachers that taught me in elementary school. To my surprise, I remembered them all.

I never thought that I had much in my life to write about. Certainly not like some authors who have had a very adventurous and exciting life. But I thought I would write some of my journey through my life for my kids because we have been separated from them quite a lot by being a pastor.

Thus, looking back over the years that God has let me live, there was more than I thought that I had to write about. Everyone has a story and a journey, whether great or small, long or short. So, I do hope the journey of my life will be a blessing to you. All Scriptures are taken from the King James Version.

Pictures thru the years

Chapters

Family Photos

Back Row: Mag, Charlie, Henry McKinley (dad), ———?, Lewis, Oscar,
Front Row: Elmer on the knee of Grandpa Henry, Lusandi (Grandma), Pless

Henry McKinnley Kuykendall 1/9/1897–2/25/1959 (sixty-two years old)
Cornelia "Nealie" Christopher Kuykendall 1/26/1904–11/15/1992
(eighty-eight years old)

The Kuykendalls originally settled in Hendersonville County, North Carolina. From there, the Kuykendalls moved out in different directions. My Grandpa Kuykendall moved to Haywood County, and that is where I was born and grew up.

Early Years

Home Place on Queen Town Rd. across from Welcome Hill Baptist Church

**Back of the old home place with the addition I built.
Back left is the old well house with red roof**

I was the youngest of six children of Henry McKinley Kuykendall and Nealie Christopher Kuykendall. I was born at home, on Queen town Road, two miles out of Canton, North Carolina. My brother Orin was the oldest, next Everett, then after him was James Alvin, then Delmar, then my sister, Mary Lou. I was called the baby of the family. I didn't like them to say that then. Now I like it because as of this writing, only two of us are left, Mary Lou and myself.

Me, Mary Lou, Delmar, James Alvin, Everett, Orin, & Mama Sitting

Me, James Alvin, Everett, Mama, Marylou, Delmar

I grew up on a small farm. Daddy had two horses that we farmed with. We always had two cows, usually two pigs, and a bunch of chickens, so I knew what it was to get up early in the morning and milk cows before I went to school, plus in the twelfth grade, I drove the school bus.

When I was not old enough to go to school, I rode with Mama to take the other kids to school. I am not sure how old I was, but I was not six years old. When the other kids got out, I pitched a fit to go with them. Of course, Mama would not let me out. As she was leaving the school grounds, I was crying, and I had a new cap on. I threw my new cap out the window. I thought Mama would stop, but she didn't. She kept on going. Mama knew how to handle temper tantrums that kids pitched to get their way.

Intersection where I threw my new hat out of the car window

Another episode to show what a wise Mama I had happened when I was in the second grade. We had a substitute teacher on this particular day, and she said she would be back tomorrow. I didn't like her, so I pretended like I was sick the next morning. Being a wise mother, she felt my forehead, and I didn't have a temperature. She knew I was not sick. She said, "If you stay out, I am going to take you and have your tonsils taken out." I didn't believe her, but lo and behold, she sacked me up and took me to our family doctor, Dr. Reeves. Back in those days, they didn't take you to the hospital. He had a back room where he took my tonsils out. He used ethereal to put me to sleep. I never laid out of school again, pretending to be sick. Mama knew how to handle kids—it is so sad that many moms don't know how to raise kids this day and time. God has provided a book to tell you how to rear children. Read the KJV Bible, especially the book of Proverbs, especially Proverbs 13:24, 19:18, 22:6, 15, 23:13–14, 29:15, 17.

Second-grade photo, Morning Star Elementary School

When I was a little boy, I tried some bad habits, but the Lord kept me from getting addicted. My mama dipped snuff, which a lot of women used back in those days. One morning when she had gone to milk the cows, I decided I wanted to try her snuff. I climbed up on the old fashion cabinet and got the snuff. I turned around and sat down on the cabinet. I pulled my lip out like I had seen her do and filled my lip full of snuff. But then I vomited it right out in the floor. That was my first and last dip of snuff. God kept me from that habit by letting me get sick.

My brother Delmar chewed tobacco, so he gave me some to try. I put it in my mouth and began to chew. I began to get sick, so I spit it out and ran to get some water to drink. I drank a lot of water. Thank you, Lord, for keeping me from that bad habit!

Another habit that the Lord kept me from was that my brother Everett smoked, and I decided I wanted to try cigarettes. He had hung his shirt over the back of a chair. I sneaked out one of his cigarettes and hid it. The next morning when Mama had gone to milk, I got the cigarette and was sitting on the oven door of the old fashion cook stove, smoking, when Mama came in and caught me. She made me smoke on my back end. So, the Lord kept me from that habit by Mama setting me on fire and God's keeping power. That was my first and last cigarette. Thank you, Lord, for keeping me from all those bad habits!

You can see the old cook stove in the background. That is the door I pulled down and was sitting on smoking a cigarette when Mama caught me.

(Picture made while still in high school)

The medical people will ask you about your habits. I said, "I don't smoke, I don't dip, I don't chew, I don't take drugs, I don't drink, and I don't even cuss. It is not that I am so good, but the Lord and Mama kept me from these things. So, moms and dads, help your kids to be clean from all these vices.

As a kid growing up, we would go to Grandmother Lusandi Kuykendall's to visit on Sunday. In those days, kids had to sit down and keep their mouths shut. Kids were not allowed to take over the conversation. That was true, not only at Grandmother's but anywhere we went to visit. Today, it is kids that take over the conversations. The parents sit and listen to their kids and laugh at the crazy things they do. How far have we gone from teaching and training kids in the way that they should go. Again, look to Proverbs 22:6, "Train up a child in the way he should go: and when he is old, he will not depart from it." Grandmother Lusandi was born on August 1, 1865, and passed away on September 27, 1951, at the age of eighty-six. Grandpa Henry Kuykendall was born on May 5, 1856, and passed away on August 2, 1928, at the age of seventy-two.

When I got big enough to carry a .22 rifle, my dad gave me one of my own. He taught me how to carry it. Always have it pointing toward the ground until you are ready to shoot at something. He said to never point it at anybody. It's not guns that kill people; it's the one who is handling the gun.

My dad had five boys, and he taught them to work. My dad was one of the hardest workers that you have ever seen. He worked at Champion Paper and Fiber Company on the day shift. When he would come home, then he would go to work on the farm. For his vacations, he would take them when the corn was ready to cut. He never took a vacation to go off to the beach or the mountains. When Dad died, some of his fellow workers said of him, "He wasted the least time of anybody in Champion Paper. He never took a smoke break or just kill time."

There was not a lazy bone in his body. To show what get up and go my dad had, when he was dating my mother, he walked across a mountain to date her. This was probably about seven miles, at least. He said there were times that he walked back across the mountain and would sleep in the gap of the mountain. He would wake up in time to walk the rest of the way home and build a fire before the rest of his family got up.

When growing up on the farm, a boy learns to do all kinds of things. I learned how to quilt from Mama. Also, I learned how to sew on a sewing machine. I sewed fringes on my pants and my shirt sleeves so I would look like "Tonto," who was on *The Lone Ranger* TV show. I would put a turkey feather on a band around my head and have my black hair parted in the middle like Tonto. Also, I used to get a cape and put it around my neck like Superman. Then I would jump out of the barn loft. But I never could fly away.

**Me in Carolyn's mom
& dad's backyard
Before we were married**

I learned how to cut up hogs. Daddy worked days at Champion Paper, so he hired a man to kill and scrape the hair off the hogs, then Nama did the cutting up of the hog. I was there to help her. Mama canned just about everything, beans, corn, tomatoes, apples, peaches, cherries, grapes, and most of the parts of the hog, like the ham, shoulders, middles, ribs, and sausage. In those days, you didn't have to run to the store to get everything; you just ran to the basement and got what you wanted to eat.

The old saying, "Jack of all trades and master of none," might be said about my life. Raised on a farm, I learned to do all sorts of things. I learned about farming and animals, like horses, cows, pigs, chickens, bees, and even rats. I learned how to be a mechanic on farm equipment and cars. I learned woodworking in high school. Also I took machine shop and learned about making things out of steel, iron, and brass. While working at Champion, I took a course in welding. Also, in high school,

I learned to type, which I do not like to do a lot of. I worked at two different service stations and learned about servicing cars.

One thing I would like to mention is we had a water bed, but we did not have a headboard for it. I decided to build a headboard for our king-sized bed. I looked

Me & Raymond Owenby
A friend from next door
helping me hoe corn

(Raymond passed away October 7, 2008, at the age of sixty-seven)

around at beds in furniture stores, then I drew up my own plans. I purchased the cherry wood, planed it, sawed it, glued it, sanded it, which is the hardest part of the job, stained it, and sprayed it with lacquer. I did it a little bit at a time. When I completed my day's work of ministry, I would work on it in my carport. I purchased the first cherry boards in 2001, and I completed the bed in 2007. Carolyn calls it the "seven-year" bed. It is all solid cherry wood. Even the drawers are cherry wood. I made six different pieces to make a complete bookcase headboard.

At the telephone company, I learned how to climb poles and install phones and trace down troubles on the line. I have done electric work and also plumbing. Also, I learned to swim at a very young age. My brothers took me with them to the Pigeon River to swim, but I could not swim. They would hold me up and let me paddle, but I still couldn't swim. One day, I was standing on a rock close to the bank. They were out in the river swimming. I stepped off the rock and went in over my head. When you go over your head in water, you will learn to swim very quickly, and so I did.

Mom and Dad never went anywhere very often, but one thing Mom and Dad did was to go to Asheville on Saturday, not every Saturday, but fairly often. Remember, we lived in Canton, so it was a nice drive. Mom and Dad never went shopping together, so I had to make a choice of which one I would go with. Daddy would go to the hardware stores and to the bridle and saddle shops, which I liked, but he would never go into a restaurant and sit down and eat. He would just get a coke and a moon pie. With Mom, it was a different story. She went to the dress stores and the shoe stores, which I didn't particularly like, but, she would always go to Woolworth's to eat. When I went with her, I would order the ham club sandwich and a chocolate milkshake. Man was that good! So I always had to make a choice, did I want something good to eat or go to the hardware and saddle shops?

That is the way it is in salvation; you have to choose between serving Christ or serving the devil, between living in sin or living a life of holiness. You have to choose between the narrow way and the broad way. You have to choose between heaven and hell. It is said of Moses in Hebrews 11:25, "Choosing rather to suffer affliction with the people of God then to enjoy the pleasures of sin for a season." Remember, there is pleasure in sin, but it is only for a season. Also, Psalm 16:11 says, "Thou wilt shew

me the path of life, in thy presence is fullness of joy, at thy right hand there are pleasures forever more." So you have to make a choice.

Me & Mary Lou

My sister Mary Lou and I were always close. When we were growing up, we were
the last two kids at home. Mary Lou and I would aggravate each other. I would be
bringing in an armful of wood for the cook stove, and Mary Lou would throw a pot
full of water all over me. She would do this especially on my birthday. She knew I
wouldn't throw the wood down to chase her. She would do this on my birthday and
say, "Happy Birthday" afterward. There were times when I would aggravate her, and
she would chase me all the way down in the corn field. She never did catch me. I ran
faster than she did.

Mary Lou, some other kids, and I were playing "Magic Circle." Mary Lou had
her eyes closed, leaning on a big oak tree in our yard. One of the kids was drawing
the circle on her back. I saw a worm on the tree, and it was not real close to Mary
Lou. I said, "There is a worm." Mary Lou started crying and ran in the house. She was
as afraid of a worm as she would have been a bear. I followed her in the house, and
Mama jerked me up and gave me a spanking before I could say anything. Mary Lou
thought I put a worm on her. Of course, I didn't. Mama took immediate action and
talked later. With correction like that, is it any wonder that I was a God-fearing and
parent-fearing kid? Mary Lou is a widow now. We are still very close. When you go
to her house, the pots and pans start rattling. She has to fix you something good to
eat when you go to her house.

My brother-in-law James Wilson

Mary Lou married James Wilson. We also became very close friends. James was

a very spiritual person. He could sing and play almost any instrument. He sang and played in a lot of church revivals. James and I went to a lot of meetings together. I remember this one church that I preached at, and after service, some folks wanted us to go pray with a man just across the street. The man had been drinking. We were talking to him about getting saved. He was angry and seemed to resist anything we said. It didn't seem like we were getting anywhere with him. I said to James, "Let us go, but before we go, let us pray again." That fellow wallowed all over the floor. But when we finished praying, he was sober and saved. He gave a very bright testimony of his conversion.

Mary Lou and James had two daughters, Deborah and Marsha and one grand-daughter, Marissa. Deborah and Marsha are the sweetest women that you will ever meet. They have certainly been good to us and also to Zion Baptist Church by sending an offering on different occasions. James passed away on March 16, 2012, at the age of seventy-six.

Lisa & James Wilson

Mary Lou & James fiftieth wedding anniversary
Left to right: Clifford & Debra Summey, Marissa Kaufman,
Mary Lou & James, Marsha & Mike McClure

My brother Orin was the oldest of all the children. My first remembrance of Orin was when I was in the yard playing as a small boy. Mama called for me to come in the house. When I went in, Orin had come in from the Navy. He was dressed in a Navy uniform, and he picked me up, and I started crying because he was a stranger to me. After Orin came out of the Navy, he married Elizabeth Hannah. They had one daughter, Ginger Ruth. Orin worked in Atlanta, Georgia, for Carolina Freight for

Elizabeth & Orin Kuykendall

most of his working career. Orin passed away on January 23, 1987, at the age of sixty-two. His wife Elizabeth passed away on October 24, 2015, at the age of eighty-five.

One time, Dennis, Hannah, and I went to visit my brother Orin and his wife Elizabeth in Atlanta, Georgia. It was the summer between the fifth and sixth grade. Dennis was Elizabeth's younger brother, and I was Orin's younger brother. Dennis and I were in the same grade in school and were good pals. We went to Grant Park every day, a 131-acre recreational park, which was only a block or so away from their house. We had a good time in the park. James Turpin, who Orin and Elizabeth rented from was employed by Georgia Power, and he did tree work on the side; trimming trees and cutting down trees. He took us with him several times to look at tree jobs that he bid on. That was a thrill, and we got to see a lot of Atlanta.

My next brother was Lucius Everett. We called him Everett. He was the tallest one in the family. He never saw a stranger. He served in the Army and was stationed in Germany. Everett married Lois Rogers. They couldn't have children, but they adopted two boys, Norris and Ivan. Everett passed away on May 1, 1997, at the age of sixty-seven. His wife Lois passed away on June 28, 2014, at the age of eighty-six.

Standing is James Alvin & Everett; sitting is Mary Lou, Mama, myself

My brother James Alvin was good-looking. He had black wavy hair and a perfect build. He was the ladies' man. He was engaged to a girl in Italy and also a girl in Andrews, North Carolina, but he didn't marry either one. Later, he married a lady by the name of Lola. Lola had two girls, Linda and Bobbie, but Lola found her another man while James Alvin was out to sea on a tour. He was in the Navy for eighteen years on the USS Intrepid aircraft carrier. The intrepid was the most hit "flat top" carrier of WWII with five kamikaze attacks and one torpedo strike. The Intrepid is now berthed on the Hudson River in New York as a tourist attraction.

USS Intrepid "flat top" carrier

While in the Navy, James Alvin went AWOL. He said he had amnesia; that was the reason he left out. He had changed his name to Johnny Rivers and was driving a tractor trailer on the base when they caught him. During the time he was AWOL, he met a girl called Ruth at a truck stop. She took him to church, and he got saved.

Growing up, we never had a TV, just a radio. One time, my brother James Alvin came in from the Navy and brought some of his furniture to our house. He had a TV that he put in the corner of our living room. But Daddy made him turn the screen toward the wall and would not let him turn it on. Daddy believed it was a sin to watch TV. Even today, at eighty-four years old, my sister Mary Lou still does not have a TV. When Carolyn and I married, we never had a TV until Odie was twenty years old. I was pastoring my second church, Zion Hill Baptist in Marion, North Carolina, when we got our first TV. Looking back on TV history, it took a while for the church to catch on that TV could be used as a powerful tool for evangelism to send the gospel to the world. Sure, the devil has used TV to promote the wickedness of the world from the beginning. But thank God, the church can use it also for the glory of God. James Alvin passed away July 5, 1992, at the age of fifty-nine.

James Alvin Kuykendall and wife Darlene Barnett Kuykendall

My brother Delmar and I were also very close. Delmar was six years older than I was. We did a lot of work on the farm together. Delmar and I used to go to the movies on either Friday night or Saturday night. We would go to the Strand Theatre and see the first feature, and then we ran as fast as we could to the Colonial Theatre and catch their second feature. One night, I went to the movies by myself. In the movie that night, two people were lying under a tree, and this black panther climbed out on a limb right over them. It was about to jump down on them. It certainly scared me. As I was walking home that night by myself, there was this sharp curve, and a big tree stuck out over the road. It was very dark and scary in that curve. I could just see a panther out on those limbs. I ran as fast as I could to get around it. Nothing ever jumped on me.

2021 Photo
This was a scary curve on Queen town Rd., which was very dark when I walked home from the movies. The big tree that overhung the road is gone.

Also, as I mention later in this writing, Delmar bought truckloads of produce, which we sold throughout communities around us. Delmar married Lelia Stewart, and they had three children, Jimmy, Karen, and Brad. Delmar passed away on August 13, 2013, at the age of seventy-six, and his son Jimmy passed away on April 19, 2021, at the age of sixty-seven.

Delmar Kuykendall

Jimmy Kuykendall

School Days

Morning Star Elementary School

I went to Morning Star Elementary School, which was about five miles away from our house. My teachers were Mrs. Walker for first grade, Mrs. Hardin for second grade, Mrs. Ellen for third grade, Mrs. Jenkins for fourth grade, Mrs. Michaels for fifth grade, and Mrs. Looper for sixth, seventh, and eighth grade.

When I was in the second grade, I failed. I took my report card home to Mama. She read it to me, "repeat second grade." I asked, "What does that mean, Mama?" She said, "It means you failed; you will have to go back into the second grade next year again." That broke my heart, and I began to cry. Mama said, "Well, you can't read." When I came out of the second grade the following year, I was the fastest boy reader in the class, and Gail Cook was the fastest girl reader. I was determined I was not going to fail again.

There is somewhat of a funny story behind Mrs. Looper. I heard before I went to sixth grade that she was the toughest teacher in the whole school. I was dreading to be in her class. When I finished sixth grade, I said, "Praise the Lord, I'm out of her class." Low and behold, if she didn't move to the seventh grade. So, I had her for the seventh grade also. Morning Star Elementary only had seven grades, and then we moved to the middle school down next to the High School in Canton, North Carolina. You will not believe this, but Mrs. Looper, who they said was the hardest teacher in Morning Star, and whom I already had for sixth and seventh grade, moved to the eighth grade! I couldn't believe it. I was going to have her for the third year in a row. I will have to say that I never had any trouble in her class. I worked hard and tried to be on my best behavior. In fact, I enjoyed her classes. She introduced our class to Yellow Stone National Park in her slides and pictures she took from her vacations there.

Elementary Years

Jeremy, King of VBS at Zion Hill

Mr. Duckett was the principal of Morning Star Elementary, and did he ever have a big paddle full of holes. He was a big, stout man and knew how to use that paddle. I got one paddling from him. I never did figure out why. Morning Star Elementary was going to go to hear an orchestra play at Canton High School. Someone asked, "If you didn't want to go, did you have to?" They said, "You had to have a note from your parents." If I remember correctly, there were three of us who brought a note so we wouldn't have to go. Mr. Duckett took us in his office and gave us a whipping—yes, a whipping because he set us on fire. I never did understand why. We brought a note from our parents that said we didn't have to go.

Canton High School

When I moved to high school, Mr. Rowe Henry was the superintendent, and Mr. W. L. Rickard was the principal. At Canton High School, different teachers taught different subjects. I will just mention a few. Some of my teachers: Mrs. Mattheson taught math, Miss Johnson—Algebra, Mrs. Mitchell—History, Mrs. Johnson—English, Mr. Holcomb—Science, Mrs. Walker—Typing, Mr. Ward—Business Education, Mr. Rhea—Machine Shop, and Mr. Wilson—Welding Shop. Doc. Wilson used to say, "The sun and moon may vary, but my watch never does." Also, he would say, "You boys are not afraid of work; you can lay down beside it and go to sleep." Mr. Bridgeman taught woodworking. His class was the last class at the end of the school day. I would stand at the door with my books, and when the bell rang, I was out of there like a bullet out of a gun.

My senior photo

Mr. Bridgeman said, "Leo, if you were on a flag pole when the bell rang, you would turn loose." I guess he was right. When school let out, I would walk home because if I rode the bus, it took an hour, and if I walked, it only took thirty minutes to get to my house. It was a two-mile walk. I did this through the eleventh grade.

While in high school, I made friends with Leroy Stevenson. We both were Christians and church-going boys. He went to the Canton Freewill Church, and I went to Welcome Hill Baptist Church. We discussed the Scriptures quite often. We disagreed on some of the doctrines that Freewill and the Baptists believed. But we were good friends. Leroy was more introverted than I was at that time. One day, he quoted something that he had read. I said, "What does that mean?" He said, "If you have a

18

chance to get married, you better take it, or you may forever remain unmarried." It was not long after that he got married. I never knew that he had a girlfriend or was even interested in girls. Thus, he took advantage of that opportunity.

I received an invitation to become a member of the Beta Club while I was in high school. I shared this with some of my fellow classmates. I said, "I am not going to join the Beta Club; that is silly." Remember, I was a country boy using country slang—taters, maters, and nanaers. If you don't know what that means, it means potatoes, tomatoes, bananas. (You can take the boy out of the country, but you can't take the country out of the boy.) My classmates said, "Oh, what an honor. You ought to join." To be a member of the Beta Club, you had to have a 90 average or above. Thus, through their urging and encouragement, I did join the Beta Club.

I had a whole Bible the size of a New Testament that I carried in my shirt pocket. Every time I got a break from my studies, I would jerk it out and read it. I read the Bible through in six months while I was at school. Those days were not bad days but good and enjoyable days. I will let you in on a secret that I don't think that I've ever told anyone. On Wednesdays, I would go out by the river, Pigeon River, which joined the school property, and fast and pray on my dinner hour. I don't remember why I chose Wednesdays, maybe because it was prayer meeting night. No one talks much about fasting today, but Paul said in 2 Corinthians 11:27, "In fasting often." If Christ, being the son of God, fasted, how much more should we fast?

What has happened to our country? When I was at Morning Star Elementary School, a preacher came in every Friday and preached in the auditorium to the whole school. How far has America gone off into infidelity? When I went to Canton High School, they had a PA system with speakers in every room. There was a devotion given every morning, a Scripture was read, and a prayer was prayed. Oh, to return to those days when the Word of God influenced young people. Further, the Gideons were allowed to give a New Testament Bible to every fifth grader. Isn't it a shame that you can't give a New Testament Bible to a fifth grader now, but when they are put in prison, you can give them a Bible? Let us return to putting the Bible back in schools instead of security guards and metal detectors. You never heard of school shootings in those days. Give them the Bible and the Ten Commandments. It is time and past time to do it.

Let me show you how far away from God America has gone. I drove the school bus the last year of high school. I put a big bumper sticker over the windshield that said, "Jesus Saves." I put another sticker over the back door that said, "Prepare to meet God." No one said to me, "You can't do that; there is separation of church and state," which is a lie; this country was founded on the Bible. The Supreme Court has a lot of blood on their hands when they took the Word of God away from generations of boys and girls. Nobody said, "You've got to take those signs off the school bus," not the principal, not any of the teachers, not the mayor, and not the city commissioners. I drove the whole nine months of the school year with those signs on my school bus. The Lord blesses his servants who fear Him and live for Him. Let me show you what the Lord did for me. I drove the oldest bus of all the school buses in the fleet. One morning, it was zero degrees, and only two buses started; one of them was mine. The rest of the buses would not start. Also, every bus in the fleet had to go to the bus garage to be worked on that year, but the bus I drove did not have to go to the bus garage the whole nine months. God blessed me, and He blessed my school bus.

**Me in front of the school bus I drove with "Jesus Saves"
over the windshieldThe White spot is a tear in the picture.**

Graduation from Canton High School

Young Christian

Sunny Point Baptist Church was the only church in our community when I was young. Sunny Point had a "split." The members that "pulled out" wanted to buy some land from my dad to build a new church on. I remember we were down in the cornfield hoeing corn when a group of men that had "pulled out" from Sunny Point came to talk to Daddy about buying land for their new church. Daddy was not saved at that time. He preached them a sermon, telling them that they needed to get together and "iron" out their differences. They didn't need to build a new church. Thus, Daddy would not sell them land. So, they bought some land almost straight across the road from our house, which was a lot better place for a church.

Sunny Point Baptist Church

Daddy never went to church in those early years, but Mama took us. Thank God for mothers who take their kids to church. Being young at Sunny Point Baptist Church, I remember going to sleep on the pew. Churches back in those days were more spiritual and very lively. When prayer was called for, everyone would kneel around the front and pray so loud that you could not hear yourself talk. I remember Mary Lou and myself walking to a Sunrise service on Easter at Sunny Point Baptist Church, and the pastor, Rev. George Ingle, stopped and picked us up. Later, Rev. Ingle had a tent revival in the Center Pigeon Community, and that resulted in starting a new church, Center Pigeon Baptist Church, which was a very spiritual church. Rev. Ingle passed away on August 12, 1995, at the age of eighty-eight.

Rev. Maurice Banks pastored Inanda Baptist Church in West Asheville, North Carolina. This is the church where Carolyn went as a young girl. In fact, Betty Banks taught Carolyn in Sunday school. Brother Banks was the pastor when Carolyn's dad got saved and announced his calling to preach. Her dad, not long after that, got a call to Antioch Baptist in Ela, North Carolina.

Maurice Banks and his wife Betty lived beside us while pastoring Sunny Point Baptist Church. I remember Rev. Banks took me and my brother fishing. We were almost ready to quit fishing and go home when I fell in the river and got wet up to my waist. I did not want to get in his car and mess it up. He said, "Ah, go ahead and get in; you are not going to hurt the car."

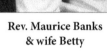

**Rev. Maurice Banks
& wife Betty**

Building Welcome Hill Baptist Church across the street was a real blessing because Daddy got saved in the first revival at Welcome Hill Baptist Church. Then, when I was thirteen years old, I got saved at Welcome Hill Baptist Church. Later, I became the custodian and cleaned the church every week. This gave me the privilege to pray and sometimes to get a song book and sing a few songs. Being alone, nobody heard how bad I sang. Further, I got to ring the church bell on Sundays and Wednesday nights.

Welcome Hill had a young boys prayer band. Every Sunday night, we had our own prayer time before service. The ages were between ten and eighteen years old. One time we had an all-night prayer meeting in a cabin on the mountain. We did not pray all night, but we did pray on and off. It was a great time for all the boys. It seems that the youth today have everything else on their minds except drawing nigh to God. Ecclesiastes 12:1 "Remember now thy Creator in the days of thy youth."

Welcome Hill Baptist Church

The first pastor of Welcome Hill was Rev. Thea Heatherly. Rev. Heatherly passed away on September 15, 1980 at the age of seventy-five. The second pastor was Rev. Zeb McDaris, under whose ministry I was saved. I remember before I got saved, when Rev. McDaris was preaching, I thought he was talking directly to me. I would try to hide behind someone sitting on the pew in front of me. After I got saved, I knew what it was. It was the Holy Spirit talking to me, convicting me of my sins. God always deals with sinners, giving them a condemning conscience. The Lord said to Saul on Damascus Road, when he was stricken down, "It is hard for thee to kick against the pricks" (Acts 9:5). The pricks are the convicting of the Holy Spirit.

In my early Christian life, I would go with Rev. Zeb McDaris to revivals, which he was preaching. Rev. Zeb worked every day at Champion Paper & Fiber Company

and also preached revivals every night. He preached a lot of revivals. Also, he pastored churches during this time. He was such a spirit-filled preacher. He could go into a church that was cold as a refrigerator, and soon they would be shouting the praises of God. Rev. Zeb would call on me, a young person, to testify. This certainly did help me to grow as a Christian. Rev McDaris passed away on September 5, 1977, at the age of sixty. I felt like he died too soon.

The third pastor was Rev. William "Bill" House, who later became my daddy-in-law.

My dad would always stand around waiting after church. If no one invited the pastor, Rev. Bill House and his family home for dinner, Daddy would say, "Come home with me." We lived just across the road. Pastor House and his family lived in West Asheville, North Carolina, and the church was in Canton, North Carolina, which was about twenty to twenty-five miles away.

Rev. Zeb McDaris
Second pastor
of Welcome Hill
Baptist Church

My sister Marylou and Carolyn, Rev. Bill House's daughter, became best friends. That is when Carolyn and I fell in love. We were married on December 20, 1957, during our Christmas break from school. I was driving a school bus, making thirty-five dollars a month when we married. That was my last year in school. We were very foolish getting married with me making no more money than that. But, as I was growing up, Daddy would give me an allowance every two weeks when he got paid. He continued to do that after I married Carolyn, giving me twenty-five dollars every two weeks. I had a great dad who was a praying dad. Sometimes Mama would have company at Daddy's bedtime. He went to bed at 7:00 pm because he got up at 4:10 am in the morning to go to work. Daddy would close his bedroom door, and you could hear him praying. It didn't matter who Mama's company was. Further, Dad was a free-hearted man. When someone came to our house to visit, Dad always wanted to give them something canned or fresh from the garden.

It is always good for an older Christian to help new converts and young Christians. When I was a young Christian, Mr. Jones pulled me aside and said, "I want

Rev. William "Bill" House
Carolyn's dad
Third pastor of Welcome
Hill Baptist Church

to loan you a book." It was titled *Dispensational Truth* by Clarence Larkin. That book put me on the right road to understanding the great doctrines of the rapture, the great tribulations, the millennial reign and the great dispensations. If every older saint would do that, it certainly would encourage young converts and strengthen the church.

Also, in those early days, I remember going on a Sunday evening up on a mountain in the Dutch Cove with Bobby Pearson and Reeves Sanford. We went up to pray. I felt so close to God that I felt if I had asked God to take me on to heaven, He would have done so. What a great experience.

It is amazing how the Lord reveals things to you after you are saved. I was a young Christian, and I passed these men on the street in Canton, North Carolina. They were asking this older man, who was a preacher, about the Holy Ghost and the Holy Spirit. He was stumbling around, trying to explain the difference between the two. I was just a young Christian. I had not been to Bible college. I had not taken Greek. I told them that the Holy Ghost and Holy Spirit were the same. I was shocked that this preacher did not know that.

When I was a young Christian, the Lord convicted me of several things. Before I got saved, I would go with my shirt off. I prided myself on having a dark suntan. After I got saved, I was in the cornfield hoeing with no shirt on. The Lord spoke to me and said, "Put your shirt on." I said, "Lord I know a preacher who goes with his shirt off." The Lord said, "I am not talking to him, but I am talking to you." It was then that I quit going with my shirt off.

I loved to swim when I was young. I loved to go swimming in the public pool in Canton, North Carolina. The Lord convicted me of going where there was mixed bathing. The Lord told me not to go back to the public pool. But I wanted to go so badly. I went against the Lord's instructions. I was climbing on the diving board, and I almost broke my foot, and the Lord said, "I told you not to go." It pays to mind the Lord.

Another occasion happened when several of the boys and myself were going to the river to swim. It was on a Sunday, and the Lord told me not to go. The Lord said, "You shouldn't be going swimming on the Lords' day." But I went on anyway. I had a new pair of shoes on. When I started to cross a barbed wire fence, I caught one of the barbs with my new shoe, and it put a hole right in top of that new shoe. The Lord said, "I told you not to go." The Lord was certainly teaching me, as a young Christian, what was right and what was wrong.

After I turned sixteen, I got my driver's license and was able to go to other churches through the week. I went somewhere almost every night except Monday night unless there was a revival somewhere. In those days, they had what is called Cottage Prayer meetings. A Cottage Prayer meeting is a meeting in someone's home. In fact, Carolyn's dad was saved in a Cottage Prayer meeting. They were great meetings, and a lot of people got saved in them. They had a Cottage Prayer meeting every week at a place called Spring Creek in Madison County. The prayer meetings in Spring Creek started at 7:00 pm and lasted until 10:00 pm. Those mountain people never got in a hurry, and they were very spiritual people. I had some buddies who went with me. We certainly enjoyed those meetings and had great fellowship with those folks.

One night, we were coming from a Cottage Prayer meeting in Spring Creek. My brother-in-law, James Wilson, was with me, along with another brother. We were coming down a long steep hill. At the foot of the hill was a very steep curve, almost a ninety-degree curve. We were talking, and I hit that curve too fast. We turned that curve it seemed like on two wheels. If we had run off the road, it was about a fifty-foot drop into a river, plus a rocky bank. The Lord has been so good to me. The Lord has spared my life so many times. Safety is of the Lord!

Another time God spared my life, Richard McDaris, Rev. Dickie Jones, and I went to Tennessee on a Saturday to visit a preacher. We stopped to visit Rev. Estel Strickland in Spring Creek, going down to Tennessee. He lived on the side of a mountain. That night, we went to his church, the Round Mountain Missionary Baptist Church in Del Rio, Tennessee, which was on a Saturday night. After service that night, we were headed to see Rev. Ballard Russel. As we were going through Newport, Tennessee, a car ran a red light and hit my car on the front fender on the driver's side. If it had been a little further back, he would have hit the door where I was sitting. That would have killed me instantly. But God had mercy and spared my life. The blow knocked my car into a service station. I can still see the plate glass window of the service station falling on the hood of my car. This happened before I was married, and I had a nice 1949 Ford. It must have addled me, for I got out preaching. A crowd had already gathered it seemed almost instantly. I am sure it must have been several minutes. Since we were out of town, the police took us to the police station to call someone to come and get us. Brother Richard McDaris called his dad, Rev. Zeb McDaris, to come and get us. You talk about being sore, I was so sore for the next day or two. The car was a total loss. The other man who hit me did not have insurance. Thank God for His mercy in sparing all three of us.

In those early days, I experienced something that no one should ever experience in church. One Sunday morning, the preacher was in the middle of his sermon when a man stood up and said, "You have slandered my family." He said a few other things and then walked out. Several other members walked out after him. The amazing thing about this was that man was an outstanding man in the church. The young people and I looked up to this man. He was a very spiritual man, and we thought we couldn't have a service if he wasn't there. The Lord taught me a great lesson that day. I was very disappointed in that man, but it did not affect my faith in Christ. I had confidence in that man, but my faith was in Christ. After that incident, my faith in Christ was as strong as ever.

Thank God for the church of our Lord Jesus Christ! But not all people in churches, regardless of the denomination, are what they profess to be. We find all kinds of people in church, loving folk, grouchy folk, arrogant folk, obnoxious folk, hateful folk, spiteful folk, complainers, gossipers, fault-finders, and doubters. But thank God for loving, humble, kind, sincere, and God-fearing folk. Remember, there are no perfect churches. When I read 1 Corinthians, even with all their faults and failures, Paul still called them saints. But people can be saved and not be perfect. In fact, there is only one perfect person who ever lived. That was Jesus Christ!

Marriage

Carolyn House & Leo Kuykendall December 1956, before we were married

School let out on Friday, December 20, for Christmas holiday. That is the day that Carolyn and I got married. Let me back up a little. I had not told Mama or Daddy that I was planning to get married. I had gone to our family physician, Dr. Reeves, to get a blood test, which you had to have to get married in those days. Low and behold, the doctor's office called and said they needed me to come back to their office. To my surprise, Mama didn't really raise a big fuss about it. She only said, "Why do they want you to come to their office?" What happened was the vial of blood they had taken from me was broken, so I had to give them more blood. The Bible says in Numbers 32:23, "Be sure your sins will find you out." On Friday night, I didn't dress up. I had on a corduroy shirt and Levi's to go get married in. I met Carolyn in the Sears Roebuck Parking lot in Asheville, North Carolina. We drove to Rev. Lones Parker's home on Pisgah Highway. He always said that "me and my wife have lived together for fifty years and never had a fight or a foot race yet." By the way, that house is still there at the time of this writing.

Rev. Lones Parker's house where we were married.

Rev. Parker had to go next door to get the neighbors for witnesses. He didn't know we were coming. I had bought Carolyn a pair of wedding rings at a jewelry store for one hundred dollars. I had to "haggle" them down to get that price. That was a lot of money in those days.

After the ceremony, I ask him how much I owed him, and he said nothing. I thanked him, and we were on our way. I didn't give him any money at all for marrying us. The Bible says in Leviticus 24:19, "As thou hast done, so shall it be done to thee." I have been paid back many times when I have married couples. I never charge couples when I marry them. Some give me money, and some don't. Rev Lones passed away on January 6, 1969, at the age of seventy-six, and his wife Minnie passed away on November 1, 1963, at the age of seventy-three.

Carolyn and I headed out on our honeymoon that night. We were going to New Smyrna Beach, Florida, where her Aunt Annie and JD lived. Mind you, we had not told them we were coming. We were foolish young people, getting married in secret, only making thirty-five dollars a month, driving a school bus, plus the money Daddy gave me to live on, and going on a long journey to see Carolyn's family, who didn't know we were coming.

To continue the story, we spent the first night in Greenville, South Carolina. On Saturday, we headed out for Florida. Neither one of us had ever been that far away from home. We were about to turn back because we thought we were never going to get there. Carolyn did not know their phone number or where they lived. All she knew was her uncle JD worked at Winn Dixie. We rolled into the Winn Dixie parking lot about dusty dark. Here came JD across the parking lot. (Was God good to foolish kids or what?) JD was glad to see us and took us home with him. We spent Saturday night and Sunday night with JD and Annie. When we woke up the first morning, I looked out the window and told Carolyn that it had snowed. It was white sand. I had never seen white sand before. Just think, snow in Florida. A foolish thought for sure.

JD and Annie, along with their three children, seemed happy that we came. One of the boys asked me to go with him to feed their pig. When we got to the lot, the trough was out from the fence about ten or twelve feet. I asked, "How do you get the feed in the trough?" He said, "You have to jump the fence," and that is what I did. When I did, the pig started running back and forth on the other side of the lot. The lot was about one hundred feet by one hundred feet. So, I poured the feed in the trough and jumped back across the fence. The boy ran back to their house and said, "Daddy, Daddy, he jumped in the lot with that wild pig." Nobody had told me that they had captured a wild pig. That boy thought I was a hero, but if I had known that it was a wild pig, I would not have jumped in with him.

JD and Annie took us to church on Sunday morning. Then on Sunday evening, JD drove us around to different sites in Florida. JD drove out on the beach to take us to see the ocean. That was the first time that Carolyn and I had ever seen the ocean. Then he took us to "The Wishing Fountain." He told us, "Make a wish before you take a drink, and it will come to pass." When I started to take a drink, I saw that the drain was green and smelled like sulfur, so I didn't take a drink. Carolyn stepped up and took a drink and said, "Shoo, that is so terrible!" It was sulfur water.

Then on Monday, we drove to Atlanta, Georgia, where my brother Orin lived. They were leaving to go home for the holidays and let us stay in their house on Monday night. On Tuesday, we drove on to Bryson City, North Carolina, to some of Carolyn's friends. We went to church with them for their Christmas play at Antiock Baptist

Church on Cooper's Creek in Ela, North Carolina. Carolyn's dad had pastored that church some years before. We drove home the next day, which was Christmas Day.

Antioch Baptist Church – Ela, North Carolina

Mama was angry at me for getting married. She did not speak to Carolyn for three days. She didn't like Carolyn at first because no girl was good enough for her baby boy. However, Mama ended up loving Carolyn probably more than all her daughters-in-law. Daddy had bought Carolyn a present and put his name only on the present. He didn't put Mama's name on the gift. Daddy didn't try to cover up for Mama.

**Carolyn & Me
Made in Carolyn's mom &
dad's backyard**

We fixed up a little house on the hill out from Mom and Dad's house. It had three rooms, no bathroom, no chimney, and no sink. I made a little homemade sink. We had about eight or ten joints of stove pipe for a chimney. One morning, we woke up, and the house was very cold. I jumped up to start a fire in the wood stove. I started the fire and threw a bunch of leaves on it, thinking that the leaves would get it going, and jumped back in bed. Instead, it filled the house with smoke. We had to jump out of bed and run outside. That is what is called "smoked out."

The road leading to the little house that we moved into was bad. So, I had a bulldozer to bulldoze a good road out to the house. Thus, it needed gravel. I had a ton-and-a-half-size truck. It looked like a dump truck, but it wasn't. So, I went and got five tons of gravel on the truck. That is all the tag on the truck was for. The five-ton of gravel plus the weight of the truck would make it overweight. If a patrolman had pulled me over, he would have given me a ticket. When I got to the driveway where I was to unload the gravel, I had an interruption. I had asked Ed Craig, our neighbor, about painting my car. Mr. Craig met me and said, "Bring your car on over. I'm ready to paint it." So, I left the load of gravel on the truck. Carolyn wanted to get the road graveled so we could get in and out because the road was red clay. When the drive was wet, it was muddy and very slick. While I was helping Ed paint my car, Carolyn shoveled off five tons of gravel by herself. She had to drive the truck forward, shovel gravel, and pull the truck forward until she reached the end of the drive. About the time we finished painting the car, she had shoveled off the last shovel full of gravel. I don't believe that I have ever seen her that angry before or since. Think about a woman shoveling that much gravel. She was exhausted plus very angry. Carolyn thought I ought to have forgotten about painting my car and shoveled that gravel off the truck. I suppose she was right, and I was a little selfish.

**Long driveway to the right is the one that Carolyn shoveled
five tons of gravel off the truck bed and onto the drive to make two routes.
The green field on the right is where I used to hoe corn.**

Carolyn was born on the Biltmore Estate in Asheville, North Carolina. It was war time, and her dad was away in the service. Later on, they moved to a home on South Bear Creek Road in West Asheville. Carolyn always had an inside bathroom until we married. Then she had to use an "outhouse." That was quite a shock to her.

After school was out, I was offered a job of mowing hay for Nelson Hinson. I look back and can't believe it. He took me up to a field where one of his employees had quit. The man left the tractor on the side of the mountain. That field was really steep, so I mowed the rest of that day. I went back the next morning and continued to mow. I started too early. There was dew still on the hay. When I started down the steepest part of the field, (steep as a mule's face), I had the tractor in the lowest gear. The tractor took off "ball hooting," that is the wheels were still turning but they had lost traction. It was really going fast. It was headed straight for a patch of woods, and I turned it to the left to try to miss the woods. The back tire raised up and sat back down. It almost turned over, which would have ended my life, but God in His mercy, spared me. He had a work for me to do in the days to come!

Later, I got a job with MO Galloway on a dairy farm in Skyland, North Carolina, milking cows in the morning and evening, farming during the day, plowing fields, and putting up hay. Mr. Galloway would cut alfalfa down one day and put it up the next. That was something unheard of on the little farm that I was raised on. Alfalfa had to dry at least four days, but Mr. Galloway had this large drying fan that dried it out. They put me on the back of the truck with a hay loader and said to keep the hay spread out. He took off, and here came the green alfalfa (heavy, heavy) continuously. It was covering me up. I could not keep all the green hay spread out.

One other incident happened on that dairy that I want to mention. Mr. Galloway had four big Hereford steer he had raised for show purposes. They had been out on the pasture and had not been "broken to lead"; that was our job. We had two ropes with four men breaking them to lead. This one Hereford, we thought we had him broken to lead. There was a driveway from the main road to the barn, probably a quarter of a mile to a half-mile long with fences on both sides. We started out that drive with this particular Hereford. Everybody turned their ropes loose for this one man to hold him. That man was stout as a mule. When that Hereford started running,

Pastor Dr. Lawrence Rhodes

that man dug in but could not hold him. All he could do was to hold the rope and hit the ground every so often. When the Hereford got to the main road, he stopped and started picking the grass. When we started back toward the barn with him, all the others turned the ropes loose, leaving me holding him. He started to run, and I dug in but could not hold him, so I was just hitting the ground every now and then. Because he was running so fast, there was no holding him. It was just like the other fellow, only this time, it was me. What a lesson to learn. Don't let sin and habits get a running start on you. Take the hoe of repentance and chop them out of your life when you first recognize them. I only worked on that dairy for three weeks. It was while living there that we visited Hoopers Creek Baptist Church, a great church and a very spiritual church. I would later in life preach a revival in that church. Rev. Lawrence Rhodes, DD was the pastor. Dr. Rhodes passed away on May 18, 2012, at the age of eighty-seven.

Family

Me, Carolyn with son Odie, daughters Sherry & Tammy

Carolyn and I have been blessed with three wonderful children—one boy and two girls. Odis Jr. was only two weeks old when he went to his first church service, and he has been in church ever since. Let me say that I dedicated my children to God before they were born. I said, "Lord, when they come to the years of accountability, I pray that they will be saved. But if they will never be saved, I pray that you let them be born dead or die as babies. I don't want my children to die and go to hell." I think as a father I had that right to pray a prayer like that.

Odie, Sherry, & Tammy

When I was a young father, I went to Tabernacle Baptist in Greenville, South Carolina to my first Sword of the Lord Conference. Dr. John R. Rice preached that night. He threw out a challenge to pray for your kids every day and to pray with them and call their names out in prayer. From that time, I started doing that. Send your kids to bed from an open Bible and a bent knee, and they will never forget it. With God taken out of schools today, kids need to be taught the Bible at home. They should hear Mom and Dad pray.

Odie, Carolyn, & me 1959

Carolyn and I went to Meadow Grove Baptist Church on Mother's Day. They were recognizing the mothers, the oldest and the youngest. Guess who the youngest mother was, it was Carolyn. So, she got the flower for the youngest mother. Odie was not even a year old at that time. She was only seventeen years old. Looking back, we were sorry she took the flower because we were visitors. Rev. Shelby Beaver was the pastor at that time.

Odie, Carolyn, me

Me holding Odie

It seems that "Odie," that is what we call him, was born full-grown. When our second child was born, Sherry Lee, Odie took care of her like a mama hen takes care of her chicks. Odie was always sports-minded. He loved to play basketball. Further, he rode in the bicycle race from Spartanburg, South Carolina, to Mount Mitchell several times, which was about 115 miles. One time, he came in third place. Also, he ran cross country. One day, he came in the house, and I said, "Where have you been?" He said, "I just ran around the circle," which was about eight to ten miles. He said, "Fix me some eggs." I said, "how many?" He said, "Five eggs." After I fixed them for him, he said, "I just ate seven before I ran." Odie has always been a big eater.

Odie with his dog Bullet

Carolyn's dad was preaching a revival in Madison County. They were eating supper with some of the folks from that church. They invited us to go. Odie was five years old at that time. We told the host that Odie did not eat much. One of the items that they had for supper was hot dogs. Odie kept asking for another hot dog. He ate five. But he didn't eat the bread, just the wienie itself. We were so embarrassed.

When Odie was about seventeen or eighteen years old, he began to let his hair grow long like a boy does at that age. Carolyn served him an ultimatum, "Either you get a haircut or move out. Your Daddy preaches against long hair on men, and you are not going to shame him." Odie said, "I'll just move out." I said, "Come here and sit down, for I want to talk to you." I said, "Don't you think it would be cheaper to get a haircut than to pay rent, pay a power bill, pay a water bill, buy groceries, and pay a telephone bill?" So, Odie got a haircut.

Odie applied and was accepted at Liberty College. His dormitory was in the middle of Lynchburg, Virginia, at that time. The new dormitories were not built on Liberty Mountain then. Odie only stayed there for two weeks when he called and wanted us to come and get him. He said, "Daddy, I can't get any sleep." He was staying in a room with four other students with one bathroom that was shared with another room of four students. Their classes started at 7:00 am. He had to get up at 4:00 am in order to get a shower and to eat breakfast and then be bused to the college by 7:00 am. He said, "Daddy, I am worn out; come and get me." Of course, we went and got him and brought him home. But Odie made it good after that bad experience. Odie went to business school. He has been a top salesman in the different car dealerships that he has worked for, such as Honda, Kia, and Chrysler. Odie is now the general manager for Marion Chrysler Dodge Jeep Ram in Marion, North Carolina.

Odie married Lisa Lavender of Old Fort, North Carolina. Odie and Lisa had their wedding at Cherry Spring Baptist Church. It was a beautiful wedding, and Odie sang to Lisa.

Odie's Wedding
Tammy, Sherry, Lisa, Odie, Me, Carolyn

Lisa & Odie

They had two boys, Jeremiah "Jeremy" and Nickolas "Nick." Odie taught his boys to work, and both of them are workers. Jeremy married Julie Hensley, and they have two sons, Grayson and Eli.

Odie has been a great blessing to Zion Hill and to Zion Baptist Church by cooking for our Labor Day Jubilees. Also, he teaches the children's church at his own church, Grace Baptist Church. He also is a good singer. Odie has always been a go-getter. Also, Odie taught his boys to be thrifty. Odie and Lisa bought Jeremy an NBA athletic coat with the Chicago Bulls and Michael Jordan's name embroidered on it when he was in sixth grade. He would rent out his athletic coat to other students for five dollars a day. So, Jeremy learned to be thrifty at a very early age. He is now a supervisor at Baxter's in North Cove in Marion, North Carolina.

Jeremy was king of VBS at Zion Hill

Nick is also thrifty. He works two jobs and sells Melaleuca products, which are nutrition, beauty, and household products. Nick married Kourtney Grindstaff on March 27, 2021. Nick built his own house before they got married. It was ready to move in when they married.

Nick & Kourtney

When Odie was a little boy, he was six or seven at that time, I bought him a cardboard guitar, but it had real strings. Also, a chord book came with it. Odie didn't take any interest in it, but I did. I learned a few of the chords, but it was a cheap guitar. A jewelry store was going out of business in Canton. I saw and bought a kay guitar for thirty-seven dollars, and that is what I learned to play the guitar on. My brother-in-law, James Wilson, taught me the chords on "What a Friend We Have in Jesus" and "Amazing Grace." Later, James found a Gibson guitar for sale. The amazing thing, I was able to buy it for one hundred dollars. It was a J50 Gibson. What a buy! While going to Tabernacle Baptist in Mt. Holly, North Carolina, the boys let me bring my guitar and play with them. I never have been able to play very well. I say that I am like an old "A Model." I miss the cord every now and then.

Bob Pitman was a number-one guitarist who I admired very much. I said, "Bob, teach me to play." I went down to his house for him to teach me how to play better. After an hour or so, Bob said, "You just better stick to preaching."

Me playing a guitar

While at Zion Hill, I never took my guitar to church to play. But after I went to Zion in Gastonia, I take my guitar on Sunday nights and Wednesday nights. I enjoy playing with the other musicians. I am still not very good, but I sound fairly well having the other players covering my blunders.

Our second child, Sherry Lee, was given two gifts. One, a gift to "gab," and the second, a beautiful singing voice. She has been singing Christian songs ever since she was little. In fact, her and Odie sang together when they were small. I would take them with me sometimes when visiting the sick and have them sing to the sick, which, to the sick, was very uplifting.

Odie, me, & Sherry

When Sherry was about ten years old, she had a very high fever. We took her to the doctor. I said, "Doc, give her a shot so it will knock it out quickly." He said, "These pills will work just as good." Well, they didn't. That night, she woke us up, seeing water running out of the wall and a red dragon. Also, she thought that Odie was putting spiders on her. Sherry was picking in the air like old people whose minds are bad. It scared the life out of us. It was about 3 or 4 am in the morning. I was the pastor of my first church, Good News Baptist, at that time. We called many of the church members

Tammy & Sherry

to pray for Sherry, waking them up. The next day, we took Sherry to her pediatrician. He gave her a ten-day shot of penicillin. Sherry got better with no after-effects. We did not know what God had done for Sherry until several years later. She had encephalitis, and most kids who have that never recover. They usually have to be put in a facility or an institution to be cared for. She has been able to live a normal life.

Sherry was the minister of music in her church for several years. What a great thing God did in answer to prayer. Doug and Sherry who live in Albana and don't come home often. When they do get to come home. I always have her to sing, and when she sings it causes me to weep, for I know what God did for her. God is a great God, one that is a miracle worker.

I always request her to sing three songs, "O What a Savior," "My Chains are Gone," and "Sweet Jesus." I've told her, "Always sing about Jesus, and you will bless folks."

When Sherry finished high school, she was accepted to Tennessee Temple College in Chattanooga, Tennessee. We took her to the college with the things she needed. We helped her get everything in her dorm. She walked out with us to the street corner. As we left, we could see her standing on that street corner by herself. You talk about hard when you leave your child alone with no friends made at that time. Carolyn and I cried for the next fifty to one hundred miles on the way home. It was hard, but we knew it was the best for her. Sherry finished college and found her husband to boot.

At Sherry & Doug's wedding
Lisa, Odie, Nick, Me, & Carolyn, Jeremy,
Sherry & Doug, Tammy

Sherry married Doug Nance of Charlotte, North Carolina. When they were going to get married, I told Sherry, "When I get through preaching on Sunday morning, come forward to be married. You have a ready-made congregation without sending out invitations." She refused that idea. In fact, I have invited other couples to do the same, but only two have taken me up on that idea.

Sherry wanted her wedding to be on Valentine's Day. I said, "That is not a good time because there may be snow." Sherry insisted on having the wedding on Valentine's Day anyway. On the night of rehearsal, it snowed like crazy. Doug, the groom, lived in Charlotte, and we lived in Marion. When it was time for the rehearsal to begin, Doug, his best man and the ushers had not arrived because of the snow. Judy Wright, who was the wedding director, began to cry because of the turmoil. Sherry was upset, but then they all made it to the church. Reservations had been made at Hook & Anchor, a fish camp, for the rehearsal supper. They called us, wanting to know if we were coming. They wanted to close because of the snow. We did go and had a good meal. I told Sherry that everything would be all right in the wedding, and it was. Their wedding went off without a hitch.

Me & Sherry on her wedding day

Jeremy was only about four years old, and he and Doug's half-brother dropped flower petals down the aisle. During the wedding, Jeremy got tired and sat down on one of the steps going up to the platform. He was so cute with his white suit and curly hair. Odie sang in Sherry's wedding. All turned out to be a great wedding.

Sherry and Doug have two children. Stephanie and Britton. Stephanie married Brooks McCullar, and they have one son, Palmer. Britton married Jamilet San Augustine, a girl from California. They have four children, Alexus, Braxton, and twin boys named Avary and Swayze.

Left to right: Me, Grayson, Eli, Jax, Braxton, Jamilet holding Avarey, Britton holding Swayze

Steffy's Wedding
Back row- left to right: Chris McCullar, Brook McCullar, Doug, Me, Odie
Front row- left to right: Stephanie, Sherry, Carolyn, Lisa

We then had a second girl, which was our third child. We named her Tamara. When Carolyn was carrying "Tammy," she was sick almost the whole nine months. I had to get oxygen and a respirator for her because she smothered. Carolyn lost weight, and her eyes sank back in her head. The doctor could not figure out what the problem was; it turned out that Carolyn should have had twins, but one did not develop. The day Tammy was born, Carolyn had put up ten dozen (120) ears of corn before she went to the hospital. After she was born, and Carolyn saw that there was

Tammy

nothing wrong with her, that she was perfect, Carolyn was so happy. I told Carolyn, "You will never be that happy again until you get to heaven." That was the happiest day of Carolyn's life because she had been so sick carrying Tammy.

When Tammy came along, she was ten years younger than Sherry, and so she was spoiled. Papaw Medford would get her anything she wanted. He loved Tammy like a father loves a daughter. If Tammy got into trouble and Carolyn had to give her a paddling, Papaw would cry. In fact, Tammy was spoiled by the people of Zion Hill. She was the youngest child that any of the pastors before me had ever had. Before Papaw's wife Mrs. Medford died, she would say of Tammy, "She is a live wire," and that she was.

One time, when Carolyn was making homemade grape jelly, it was boiling hard, and Tammy said, "I want to get saved." Carolyn said, "Can't you wait till it gets done?" Tammy said, "No, I want to get saved right now." Carolyn cut the boiling jelly off and prayed with Tammy, and she got saved. Jesus said in Matthew 19:14, "Suffer little children, and forbid them not, to come unto me: For of such is the kingdom of God."

A funny experience happened when Tammy was about three years old. I took her with me to a plumbing business. While I was talking to the clerk, Tammy said, "I need to use the bathroom." I said, "Wait just a minute." When I was through talking to the clerk, I said to her, "Let me take you to where the bathroom is." Tammy said, "I have already used it." I said, "Where?" She said, "In the commode," pointing to a display commode in the showroom window. It was beside a busy street. Being three years old, when she saw the commode, she thought it was for her to use. I wonder what people thought when they saw her sitting on a commode that was there for display in the showroom.

Tammy

When I went to Zion Hill Baptist, they had a singing every second Saturday night. Carl Hensley and Tammy were always the first people to be at the church. We lived right beside the church. This was the first singing we had when I became the pastor

Me, Carolyn, & Tammy

of Zion Hill, Tammy came running back to the house, thrilled to pieces. She said, "Mother, there's not going to be any preaching tonight, only singing." She thought that was really something. She was so happy about that. One Sunday while I was preaching, Tammy asked Carolyn, "Is he about to the bottom?" What she meant was if I about at the end of my sermon.

While Tammy was still little, she would whisper and invite folks to come over after church and have cake and coffee. However, there was no cake! Carolyn always had coffee. But Tammy took it upon herself to invite folks to our house.

Tammy used to say, "When I get grown, I am going to dance, dance, and dance." I don't know where she got that because Carolyn and I never did dance. But I found out why she never pursued dancing. Carolyn told her, "Tammy, dancing caused John the Baptist to get his head cut off," and that put the fear of God in her heart, and Tammy renounced dancing.

Tammy is the only one of my kids that has taken any interest in my books. I have a tremendous library, more books than I could ever read. I figure if I get one thought out of a book, it has paid for itself. I sometimes ask people what is the first thing they do with a new book. They give different answers. I tell them I put my name right inside the cover and the date I bought it. Also, I put the date that I read a certain portion. I have been reading the Bible through every year for years. I always date the place where I stop reading. It is surprising to look back in some of the books that I have read and see the time that I have read a chapter or a paragraph. And it may have been twenty or thirty years since I have read that particular portion.

Tammy married Jeff Dulaney, and they had two boys, Brandon and Jeffrey.

Tammy's sons Brandon & Jeffrey

Tammy with sons Brandon & Jeffrey

Brandon married Shannon Long, and they have two children, Jax and Roxie. Jeffrey married Tasha Boler, a girl from California. He was in the Air Force stationed in California. Also, Britton was in the Marines stationed in California. So, they both ended up marrying girls from California. Jeffrey and Tasha have two kids, Tatiana and Jace. Jeffrey was a recruiter for the Air Force for several years.

Roxie, Shannon & Jax

Shannon, Brandon, Tammy, Jeffrey

Later, Tammy married John Pannell. So, our family has grown. We have four generations now. We may never live to see five generations, but thank God for our family. As far as I know, all of our family who are old enough are saved.

John Pannell, Tammy, & Carolyn

Family Photos

Left to right: Britton, Jeremy, Nick, Carolyn, & me, Brandon

Back row – left to right: Brandon, Tammy, Shannon, Odie, Nick,
Jeremy holding Grayson, me
Front row – left to right: Carolyn, Lisa, Julie

Dedication of Eli

Left to right: Sherry, me, Odie, Tammy

Left to right: Shannon (Brandon's wife), Jeffrey, & Brandon

Standing: Lisa, Odie, Nick, Brandon, Tammy, & Jeffrey
Sitting: Me, Carolyn, & Bobbie Kay Tark

Job Experiences

Looking back to some of my job experiences, as I stated earlier, my first job after I graduated from high school was cutting hay for Nelson Henson. Then I worked on MO Galloway's farm. The amazing thing about that farm is that Duke Power bought the farm and put Lake Julian, located in Arden, North Carolina, where the farm used to be. This is a 300-acre lake. Later, I worked at two different service stations. I got a job at the GE plant in East Flat Rock, North Carolina. I drove a fork lift, unloading products that came in. The worst part of the job was the day that sand came in for sand-blasting. The bags weighed sixty to one hundred pounds each, and every one had to be lifted by hand. Later on, they came in on a pallet, which was so much better. The weather was rough in the winter months because there was always a draft on the docks. GE was where I worked until I got on at the Champion Paper Plant in Canton, North Carolina. My Grandpa Christopher helped drive the piles for that plant. My dad worked there for thirty-five years. My brother Delmar also worked there for a while.

Champion Paper Mill

I had to work shifts, which I didn't like, having to miss church on Sunday morning for the day shift and on Sunday evening on the 3:00–11:00 pm shift, and on the grave-yard shift, I had to miss Sunday morning service to sleep. After four years, I was laid off. Not for any fault of mine but because they had plant-wide cutbacks by seniority.

My dad died just after I began working at Champion. I had worked seven days straight, which went from Monday through Sunday. The 3 to 11 pm shift started on Wednesday at 2:30 pm. I had gone in on my first 3 to 11 shift when I received a call, saying, "Your dad is sick." When I got home, I found out that Dad had died in the hospital about 7 or 8 o'clock. I ate dinner with him that day before I went to work, and he seemed just fine, but after I went to work on my first 3 to 11 shift, Dad got sick and was taken to the hospital, where he died. Hebrews 9:24 says, "It is appointed unto man once to die and after that the judgment." I thought that he died too young at sixty-two years old. I was only nineteen years old, and my first child, Odie Jr. was only three months old when Daddy died. It was a great loss.

Side photo of Champion Paper

Dad had a unique gift. He could see a rabbit sitting in their nest. He never did a lot of rabbit hunting. One day, he came into the house and got his rifle. He said he saw a rabbit out in the edge of the woods. I went with him. I begged him to let me shoot the rabbit. I was about ten years old. Dad said, "Okay." I said, "Where is he?" He said, "He is right there," pointing to where the rabbit was. I said, "Where?" I couldn't see the rabbit. He blended in with the leaves so good. Daddy said, "Give me the gun," and when he shot the rabbit, I saw it then. Dad must have had sharp eyes, for he could find more things along the road that had fallen off of vehicles, just driving along. I certainly never could see that well.

Still further, Dad taught me much about mechanics because he worked on Ford A Models a lot. In fact, he built one by buying different parts and building it from the frame up. After Dad died, I overhauled three different vehicles. First, it was a 1949 Ford tractor. After, I started overhauling the Ford tractor that we had on the farm. My brother-in-law saw the tractor all torn apart, and he said, "You will never get it back together again." But to me, it was so simple. After that, I overhauled a 1953 Ford truck and also a 1954 Chevrolet truck.

I worked at Champion Paper and Fiber Company for about four years. The night that I was laid off, some of the Christian brethren went out on the roof and prayed during the dinner hour, which they did quite often. I went with them that night. I felt like it was my coronation day, even though it was my last shift, and I owed money that I had borrowed at the company credit union, which was about $1500–$2000. That was a lot of money back then. David said in Psalm 37:25, "I have been young, and now am old; yet have I not seen the righteous forsaken, nor his seed begging bread." I knew the Lord would take care of us. Champion has since been sold and is now called Blue Ridge Paper.

Champion Paper Mill

There is a story I must insert here. After I was laid off, Jarret Lee Howell and I went down through South Carolina, Georgia, and Florida, putting in our applications for jobs. On our journey, we spent one night in Augusta, Georgia. We stayed at an old boarding house with just one bathroom for the whole floor. I remember going to the bathroom and getting on my knees and praying and asking the Lord for a job. He gave me the assurance that He was going to give me a job. We made the round with no luck.

When back home, Mom and I went to Atlanta, where my brother Orin lived. He worked for Carolina Freight, and I put my application in there. Then I went to Atlanta Transit to put in my application; they gave me a lie detector test. It looked like I was going to be hired there for sure, but when I came out to the car to leave, my sister-in-law Elizabeth said they had called from home and wanted me to be back home the next day. It turned out to be Southern Bell that called, wanting me to be at their office the next day.

Me in front of the Southern Bell work van

I worked seven years for Southern Bell. I was hired in Asheville and sent to work in Charlotte with Southern Bell. I started working on the Monday after Easter Sunday in 1963, and my last day was April 11, 1970, when I went into full-time ministry. We lived in an apartment on Belhaven Blvd across from the A&P store for six months, and then we moved to Mt. Holly, North Carolina. After about nine months, we transferred back to Asheville, North Carolina with Southern Bell.

Me while working for Southern Bell

When we moved to Charlotte, North Carolina, I rented a truck in Asheville, North Carolina, and drove to Canton, North Carolina, to get our furniture. My brother-in-law, James Wilson and Kenneth Bennett helped me move. When we got to the apartment in Charlotte, there was no power on. We had to carry everything in by the light of a streetlight. We just carried stuff in and sat it down. It was the day before Easter. We got back to Canton at 1:00 am in the morning. The next evening, which was Easter, Carolyn and the kids, only Odie and Sherry at that time, and I traveled to our new home in Charlotte, North Carolina. We set up a bed for us and one for the kids. The next day was my first day of work at Southern Bell. When I came home from work that evening, Carolyn had everything in place.

One morning, while living in the apartment, Carolyn came running into the bedroom and said, "The stove is on fire." I jumped up and ran into the kitchen, and smoke was coming out of one of the controls. It was an electric stove with the push button switches. The rest of the stove still worked. I told Carolyn, "Don't use that eye anymore." A few mornings after, she came running into the bedroom again and said, "The stove is on fire," and sure enough, it was. Flames were coming out of the push button switch, so I put it out. The kitchen stove would not work after that. Since we didn't have enough money to buy a new stove, I went and bought a Coleman two-eye gas stove like you use when you're camping. Carolyn cooked all our meals on that stove for two weeks. One day, it dawned on me to check the breaker box. Low and behold, it was one of the long fuses that had blown. I put a new fuse in, and the stove was good except for that one eye. I put duct tape over that switch so Carolyn would not use it again, and we used that stove for several years after that.

While living in Charlotte, we joined the Tabernacle Baptist Church in Mt. Holly, North Carolina. The pastor was Rev. Hardy Medlin. The church has since changed its name to Way of the Cross Baptist Church. Rev. Bobby Meeks is the pastor at present.

While at Tabernacle Baptist, we made some great friends. Noah and Ruth Heath took us under their wings, and that was such a blessing to us. We only went there for two weeks, then joined. We met Jack Nettles, Wylie Pool, Bob Pittman—a great guitarist (to me, he could play better than Chet Atkins), Rev. James and Virginia Wooten, and Rev. Ken and Margaret Spirlin. Also Mr. and Mrs. Loftis were all our great friends until they died.

When we accepted the call to Zion in Gastonia, Virginia, Wooten came and joined Zion. She told us that she had prayed for the Lord to send us back down there after all those years that we had moved back to the mountains from Charlotte. I said to her, "The Lord answered your prayers." Virginia Wooten passed away on December 30, 2003, at the age of eighty-one.

Carolyn, me, & Virginia (Jenk) Wooten
Jolly Seniors dinner in Zion Fellowship Building

Rev. Ken and Margaret joined Zion after I became pastor there. They were members there until they passed away. Rev. Ken passed away on January 7, 1996, at the age of sixty-seven, and his wife Margaret passed away on January 24, 1997, at the age of sixty-three.

I preached my first revival at Tabernacle Baptist Church, also my first funeral. Further my first baptismal sermon was at a baptizing on the banks of the Catawba River, even though I had not announced my call to preach at that time. At Tabernacle Baptist, we enjoyed worshiping with those folks tremendously.

I remember being on the platform at Tabernacle Baptist and playing my guitar with the musicians. The pastor was giving the invitation, and the Lord pointed out this lady. I could tell she was under deep conviction. I laid my guitar down and walked back to where she and her husband were sitting. I spoke to her husband first, and out he came, and she was right behind him and down to the altar; they went and got saved.

There were other times this same thing has happened. When we were giving the drama "I Dreamed I Searched Heaven for You," as the pastor was giving the invitation, I could see conviction all over this particular man. So, I went to him and just stuck out my hand, and down in the altar he went and got saved.

On another occasion, I was preaching a revival in this particular church. This one man evidently had been prayed for a long time. In the invitation, several different brethren went back to him. Even his son went and talked to him. Then I was impressed to go speak to him. I said to him, "If you are ashamed to go to the altar, just bow right here."

He said, "No, I am not ashamed." Then I said, "Let's go to the altar." He bailed out and went to the altar and got saved.

Sometimes people just need a little encouragement. But I do not recommend you do that unless you are led by the Holy Spirit.

I was preaching a revival in another church. In the invitation, I could see the pianist was under conviction. I waited to have the people to stand to sing, giving her time to respond to the invitation. I finally said, "Let us stand and sing." She came to the piano and began to play. But before the invitation ended, she left the piano and went to the altar and had her need met. People need to respond to the Holy Spirit.

Moved Back to the Mountains

We moved back to Asheville from Mt. Holly and lived on Dogwood Dr. off Brevard Road. Then we moved in with Mama so I could build a bathroom in her house, which she never had. Daddy had passed away, and they never had a bathroom at all, only outhouses. I had never built anything like that before, so I dug the basement out as much as it needed, then I laid the blocks, which I had never laid blocks before. I had watched masons laying blocks. I didn't do such a great job, but they looked fairly well. The worst part of the job was the shingles on the roof. When you are on a roof, you are always in a strain. Of course, after a while, I got it built.

Later, Carolyn and I moved up to Medford Branch Road, off Pisgah Highway in Candler, North Carolina.

My mountain house in Candler

Wild Cow

As young parents, having to feed a family, we had a freezer to put vegetables and beef in. I would raise my own beef to kill and eat. I went to what is called in Asheville, "The Stock Yard," where they sold cattle. I didn't really know how to bid when they were selling the cattle. I ran into a friend who I went to church with. He told me that anything I wanted, he would bid on it for me. Thus, I bought a 1,000-pound white-faced cow. I didn't have a truck, so he told me he would haul her to his place, and then I could come and get her later.

The next week, I went to his place to get the cow. He said that she was so wild that when he tried to put her in the barn, she would run to the top of the mountain. A few days later, he came driving up with her in his truck. I had bales of hay under the barn that blocked the stall where I wanted to put her. So, I moved the hay and left a few bales so that she could walk off the truck right into the stall. Instead of going in to the stall, she crawled over all the hay, and out into the open pasture she went. The

54

only problem was my fence around the pasture was not good. As a result, she ran all over the community for two weeks. Some of the local fellows who rode horses said, "We will catch her for you." But she was so wild that they could not catch her. The cowboys that couldn't catch her said, "You just as well shoot her." I said, "If I do, she will not be fit to eat." I said, "I'm going to catch her."

I was working at Southern Bell at the time. It was Veterans Day, and I was off. I said I was going to catch that cow today. So, I got my rope and a box with horse feed in it. I went over to the woods where she had been staying much of the time, close to the neighbor's cows. She wasn't there. After looking for her a little while, I went back to the house. After lunch, it began to snow. I looked out of a window, and there she was, running up the road. I grabbed my rope and box of feed and took off. The snow had already covered the grass, so she was having a hard time getting something to eat. When I caught up with her, I set the box of feed in front of her. She started eating it. I tried to throw the rope over her head, but she would shake it off and back up a short distant. So, I put the loop around the box of feed. But one thing I did that saved the day was that I tied the other end of the rope around a small tree. When she came up and started eating, I flipped the loop over her head and tightened it up. She lunged and jumped. I thought she was going to pull that tree out of the ground. She finally wound herself up in the rope and fell over. With help, I was able to get her in the barn. After about six weeks of being stall-fed, she was a lot tamer. The moral of this story is to persevere. Don't quit, don't give up, be patient, and keep your eyes on the prize. If I had shot her before I caught her, the meat would not have been fit to eat.

Mount Pisgah in the far distance.
Photo taken at an intersection to my home
Bible reference to Mt. Pisgah, Deuteronomy 3:27 & 34:1

After we moved to Medford Branch Road, we joined Mt. Pisgah Baptist Church—Rev. Bill Belcher was the pastor. Rev Belcher was a great preacher; he also was a great pastor. He could build a church; further, he was great at preaching on "types." He could take one word and preach all day, it seemed. He was a man who wanted to start on time. If the song leader was not there or was late, he would jump up and say, "Turn to page so and so, and let us stand and sing." Rev Bill Belcher and his wife Clara had two children, Carolyn and Ralph. Carolyn was a tremendous pianist. She married Alfred Dunn, who could sing like a mocking bird. Ralph later announced his call to preach and became a pastor.

Mt. Pisgah Church, where I was ordained

Rev. Belcher organized a group from the church, and we went to different churches to put on "I Dreamed I Searched Heaven for You," a very stirring and touching drama. There were about seventy people who went every Saturday night to give the drama. We went to churches in South Carolina and Tennessee and, of course, all over Western North Carolina. Carolyn sang in the trio that did the singing in the program. I had the part where I came in preaching, and the devil would come and try to get me to go back. I would say to the devil, "Get behind me." I had the privilege of preaching up and down the aisles in a lot of churches. Of course, I went on in to heaven in the program. There were a lot of people saved through that drama.

Me & Rev. Bill Belcher

While we were attending Mt. Pisgah, I asked Rev. Belcher if he would like to go and hear a converted Jew preach, by the name of Dr. Godsey. He said that he would like that very much. Dr. Godsey was preaching at Beulah Baptist Church in Leicester, North Carolina. I thought I knew where the church was at, but I was wrong. We went to the wrong church at the outset. Then, we stopped on the main road and inquired at a house as to where the church was at. So, they told us how to get to the church. I was wrong about something else. I thought the service started at 7:30 pm. When we got to the church, we went in and sat down. Dr. Godsey was at the pulpit and said, "That's it!" The service was over. Rev. Belcher began laughing; for him, it was so funny that we got there when the last "Amen" was said. I was glad that he laughed about it instead of being angry with me and blessing me out. I so wanted him to hear that converted Jew preach. I had already heard Dr. Godsey preach before.

My good friend, Rev. Charles Worley, was raised and taught to believe the amillennial doctrine. To my surprise, Rev. Worley had Dr. Godsey, the converted Jew to preach at the Church where Rev. Worley pastored. Dr. Godsey showed Rev. Worley the light of the premillennial doctrine. That was a great blessing to Rev. Worley. I told Rev. Charles that God had really used him. But if he hadn't seen the light, he would be sitting on the side of one of those mountains doing nothing. But God has greatly used him as a pastor and also as an evangelist. That is where I first heard Dr. Godsey speak, at his church.

Me & Rev. Charles Worley

During my stay at Mt. Pisgah, God was calling me to preach, but I wouldn't announce it, even though I had done quite a bit of preaching. Also, they elected me to teach the men's Sunday school class. I did a lot of growing sitting under Rev. Bill Belcher. Rev. Belcher passed away on January 5, 2004, at the age of eighty-nine.

I remember being in the pasture cutting briars on the little place we had bought, and the Lord was saying to me, "You don't need to be doing this, but you should be winning souls." I had said to the Lord, not sure that God wanted me to preach, "I moved up here in the boon docks, and if you want me to preach, you will have to crowbar me out," and that is exactly what He did. I was soon preaching up and down those church aisles, also teaching the men's Sunday school classes; then came the call to preach at Good News Baptist. God knows where you are at. He knows how to reach you. It has bloomed into being the pastor of three churches.

Rev. Belcher, wife Clara, & daughter Carolyn

(1). Good News Baptist in Candler, North Carolina
(2). Zion Hill Baptist in Marion, North Carolina
(3). Zion Baptist in Gastonia, North Carolina.

Announced call to preach at a Cottage Prayer meeting in this house

God's plan for our lives is so amazing. When we lived in Charlotte, and I was working with Southern Bell, we would go up Highway 74, going back home to see our parents in Canton and also West Asheville. I remember seeing the sign for Gardner Webb College. I never dreamed that one day I would attend and graduate from that college.

Another occasion, after we transferred back to Asheville, I was sent to bury a telephone line to a new church that they were building, by the name of Good News Baptist. Several of the members were inside painting. There were no pews in the church at that time. I never dreamed that I would be the second pastor. The first pastor only stayed there about a year or two. God's plan is so amazing. Things that you would never dream of, God brings them to pass. "His ways are past finding out." Rom. 11:33

Papaws

Over a period of nineteen to twenty years, we took in three papaws. When we moved to the South Hominy Community, we met Mr. Mack Medford and his wife Bessie, who lived above us. They went to a Methodist church. In the course of time, I asked Mr. Medford if he was a Christian, if he was saved. He said, "No," even though he went to church occasionally and even tithed. So, I would take him to revivals when I got the chance. I took him to hear Dr. Percy Ray, who was preaching a revival at Ebenezer Baptist Church in Hendersonville, North Carolina. I took him right up on the front seat. He didn't want to sit there, but I said, "Papaw, nobody knows you are here." Dr. Ray preached a hair-raising sermon that night. In the invitation, Dr. Ray came and spoke to Papaw, but he didn't respond. On Sunday night, at Mt. Pisgah Baptist Church, where we attended, I got Papaw to go. They gave an Easter play, which I was in. When the invitation was given, I was praying for him, and I said "Lord, is Papaw Medford never coming forward?" I looked up, and there he came and got saved. That was a happy time.

First Papaw – Mack Medford

Sometime after Mrs. Medford died, we asked Papaw Medford to come live with us. At that time, we had moved to Marion, North Carolina, and I pastored Zion Hill Baptist Church. Papaw Medford agreed, and he came to live with us, which turned out to be nine years. He went almost everywhere I went, hospitals, visitations, revivals, funerals, and even vacations. This was a man that they wanted to put in a nursing home. But God let him enjoy nine years of traveling with us after his wife died. Some people are thrown away before their time. Before she died and before he came to live with us, he was in the Aston Park Hospital. Mrs. Medford called me and asked me to visit him in the hospital in Asheville. She said the doctors wanted to put him in a nursing home. She wanted me to see what I thought about him. I went to visit him.

He could not understand anything I said. He was deaf in one ear and had to have a hearing aid in the other. I looked at his hearing aid; the battery was missing. I found it under his pillow. I put it in his hearing aid, and then he could understand me. He said "Preacher, they will kill you here. I wanted to get up to use the bathroom, and they held me in the bed. I couldn't understand a thing they were saying, and they couldn't understand me, so I just wet the bed." I called Mrs. Medford and told her to take him home, and he would be alright. And he was alright when he got home. Later, he came to live with us after his wife died. Papaw Medford was the hardest working little fellow that you would ever saw. That is one reason why he was so close to me. He would help me dig my potatoes and get leaves for my calf. Anything I had to do he was more than willing to do it. We had some great times with him.

One funny event took place at "Camp Zion," Dr. Percy Ray's camp in Myrtle, Mississippi. Papaw Medford and I were attending the camp meeting. Their dormitories would sleep 600 people. There were four bunk beds pushed together; the aisles were leading to the bathrooms in the middle of the dormitory. Papaw Medford had gotten up to go to the bathroom in the middle of the night. The lights were out. On his way back, he missed our aisle. He was waking everybody with his flashlight, shining the light in their faces. I woke up with Papaw saying, "Do you know Leo Kuykendall?" which no one knew me because they came to Camp Zion from all over the USA. I jumped up and got Papaw and took him back to his bed.

Men's dormitory at Camp Zion in Myrtle, Mississippi

Another funny experience we had with him, though it wasn't funny then. Papaw was with us on vacation in Florida. We had stopped at this motel on the side of I-95. There were two motels side by side. Sherry and Tammy had gone to the swimming pool, and Papaw went to keep an eye on them. After a while, the girls came back to the room without Papaw. We asked, "Where is Papaw?" They said, "He was supposed to come back to the room." So we went out and began looking for him. There was an unpaved street between the two motels. I went to the other motel after looking everywhere. He had gone to the wrong motel asking for me. Of course, they didn't know me or him either. That was a scary time being that far from home and someone getting lost.

Also, Papaw had this little saying right before he went to bed every night, "If you need me, ras (roll) me out." He just didn't say it, he meant it. Further, he thought when my Honda rolled, that's what I drove, and he ought to be in it. Still further, as I said, he was a working man. He would see someone running on the side of the road, and he would say, "I would like to get behind them with a withe (a switch), then they would run, or what they need is a mattock and go to work." He thought they ought to be working instead of running. He certainly believed in work. The Bible does too. (See scriptures below) Papaw Medford passed away on January 12, 1987, at the age of eighty-one. His wife Bessie passed away on October 6, 1977, at the age of seventy-two.

Scriptures on work

1. In the sweat of thy face shall thou eat bread, 'till thou return unto the ground." Genesis 3:19
2. In all labour there is profit: but the talk of the lips tendeth only to penury" (poverty, need, want) Proverbs 14:23.
3. this we commanded you, that if any would not work, neither should he eat." II Thessalonians 3:10.
4. and to work with your own hands, as we commanded you." I Thessalonians 4:11.
5. that with quietness they work, and eat their own bread." II Thessalonians 3:12

Second Papaw

The second papaw was Carolyn's dad, Rev. Bill House. Carolyn's mother, Vervena, had passed away, and Carolyn asked her dad to come and live with us. He had a stroke when he was about fifty-four or fifty-five years old. He had to have a brace on his left foot to be able to walk. He had to swing his left arm. But he had taken care of Carolyn's mother until she died. Both of Carolyn's parents were outgoing. Her mother was always laughing. Her dad, before he had the stroke, was a powerful preacher. He was a mountain preacher. When he closed his sermon, he would be wet with sweat. He didn't give invitations as most preachers. He would say, "Let us stand and sing." He would go back and talk to sinners, inviting them to come forward. He was a great soul winner. When he came to live with us, he certainly made things lively. He loved to call people on the phone and spend time talking with them. He was always asking people personal questions. He knew more about my members than I did, in a lot of cases. He was a strong prayer warrior, seeing many of his prayers answered. He lived with us about three years before he died. I was pastoring Zion Hill in the years that he lived with us. He went with me and Carolyn when I preached a weekend meeting at Zion Baptist. I guess it would have been trial sermons. When we pulled out of the parking lot of the last night, he said, "When are we coming?" He was sure that Zion was where the Lord wanted me. Carolyn and I went on a vacation in November 1993. While we were gone, her dad had to go to the hospital. He was staying with Carolyn's sister Sandy Whitaker while we were away. He was still in the hospital when we moved to Zion Baptist in Gastonia, North Carolina.

I came to Zion on December 12, 1993, and on the second Sunday, which was December 19, 1993, they called and said that Carolyn's dad had died. So he never got to come with us to Gastonia, but he would have loved Zion.

Left to right: in the back is Jeremy & Nick Kuykendall
Front row: Bill House, Jeffrey, & Brandon Dulaney

Before Carolyn's mother died, we lived in Marion and Carolyn worked at Hanes in Morganton, which was thirty miles from home. Carolyn worked ten hours a day and a half-day on Saturday most of the time that she was employed there. Carolyn drove up to Candler in the evening time, spent the night, and would leave out at 4:00 am to drive back to Marion, get ready for work, and drive to Morganton to work at Hanes. She had to be at work at 7:00 am. She sat up every third night with her mother for a year because she had pancreatic cancer.

I would like to share a story that shows how God blesses his children. Before Carolyn's mother died, she was in the hospital in Asheville, and Carolyn's dad was staying with us while she was in the hospital. On this particular morning, there was snow on the ground, so I took Carolyn to work. Cars and trucks were all over the place. Some were in the median, and some were off the side of the road. I was driving a Honda Civic and had no problem driving in the snow. When I got back home, I took Carolyn's dad to Asheville to be with his wife "Pug" (her nick name), who was in the hospital. When we got to Black Mountain, the Richard Petty Bridge was blocked by a tractor trailer truck. We had to go through the town of Black Mountain. When I was coming back

Carolyn's mother Vervena
House in Florida

home, remember that Interstate I-40 was covered with snow and was slick. I got to the foot of the mountain at Old Fort, North Carolina, and here came a van across the bridge and slid off into the median and then turned over on its top. I pulled over and asked the man that was crawling out, "Are you hurt?" He said, "No." I asked, "Is anyone else in the van?" He said, "No." I said, "Come on, and I will take you to the service station to call someone." He said, "I can't leave the scene of an accident." I told him, "There was no one else involved." I knew that someone else would be coming across that bridge and might slide into his van. That almost happened just as I thought. Here came a car sliding off into the median and hit the guard rail but did not turn over and did not hit his van but was very close. The lesson is this, God had let me drive sixty miles to Morganton and back and also eighty miles to Asheville and back with no slipping and sliding. God is so good! Rev. House passed away on December 19, 1993, at the age of seventy-two. His wife, Vervena, passed away on February 20, 1990, at the age of seventy.

Third Papaw

Grady Edwards was the third Papaw who came to live with us. Carolyn's family and the Edwards lived side by side when she was growing up. Geneva Edwards was their daughter, and she and Carolyn were like sisters. Geneva and her husband Ashely Todd and their three-month old baby Melisa were killed in an accident on Interstate 85 near Lexington, North Carolina, on November 14, 1963. Geneva was only twenty-four years old. Carolyn stepped up to help Grady and his wife Ollie Edwards. She took them to the doctors and helped them fill out papers that they needed to fill out. Carolyn even painted the inside of their home several times because Mr. Edwards was a chain smoker, and everything in their house was yellow from cigarette smoke. That smoking got him in trouble. He had surgery of the colon; it was cancer. Then later he had cancer of the throat. After that surgery, he quit smoking cold turkey. Afterward, his wife Ollie passed away on February 25, 1996, at the age of eighty-two. Carolyn asked Mr. Edwards to come and spend a few days with us, which turned out to be seven years. When he came to live with us, he didn't want to go back home. Further, he loved to go to Market Street Buffet. He was always a big eater. When we first started taking him there to eat, he would get five different desserts. One lady said, "He's not going to eat all those, is he?" Carolyn told her to "watch him." Later, he only got one. I think he got ashamed of eating so many desserts.

Third Papaw–Grady Edwards

There is a funny story about his love life. When Papaw Edwards started coming to Zion, he said of all the widows, he only liked Virginia "Jenk" Wooten. So he started sitting beside her in church. One day, we went out to eat with David and Pat Spirlin and Sandra Brittain. Sandra got Papaw by the arm and began to sing "You not woman enough to take my man," just going on with him. Papaw fell in love with Sandra. He didn't want to walk with "Jenk" out to the Fellowship Building after that. Papaw requested Sandra, who sang with the Faith Trio, to sing a certain song at service. She didn't sing that song, so he got mad at her and would not speak to her.

After this, Papaw Edwards liked one of the waitresses at Market Street Buffet, whose name was Joann. He even gave her money for her birthday, which was unusual because he was very tight with his money. One day, she came and touched him on the shoulder and said, "How are you today, Grandpa?" That was the wrong word. He was thinking of her more like a girlfriend. That was the end of him liking her. Still further, one day, one of the younger waitresses said, "Papaw, why don't you marry me?" He misunderstood what she said. He thought she said, "Are you ever going to get married again?" He said, "No." When we got out in the car, I said, "Papaw, you got a marriage proposal. She asked you to marry her." He said, "She did?" I said, "Yes." So every time that we went back to eat at Market Street, he would look for her. Then, I found out she was expecting a baby. When we got in the car that day, I said, "Papaw, just think, if you had married her, you would be a new daddy." I guess that was mean of me. After that, I could hardly get him to go back to Market Street to eat. He really thought she meant it about getting married. You must remember, he was eighty-eight years old, and she was about twenty years old. It is something how he would set his affections on different people and how easily he would turn against them.

One time, Papaw Edwards and I were leaving Market Street Buffet. When we got to the sidewalk, there was a high curb, and Papaw was afraid of that high step. So, I got him by the arm, and I said, "Papaw, just one jump like a rabbit, and you will be down." Just then, I heard his feet drag, and down he went. His knee landed on my left foot, which broke his fall. Later, he told Carolyn that I pushed him down. She said, "Why is Leo's foot blue where you fell on it?"

He certainly was an unusual man. He was pre-diabetic, but he would eat sugar like it was going out of style. He would put two or three spoon full of sugar in sweet tea. He had to have one of the white sugar-covered cinnamon buns every day. The greasier the food, the better he liked it. He did everything that doctors tell you not to do. Papaw passed away on November 12, 2002, at the age of eighty-eight years old. He lacked three months before turning eighty-nine. I told Carolyn that when he died, we should have donated his body to science to see what he was made of.

Pastoring Good News

My first church
Good News Baptist Church

On the road of pastoring, it was on a Saturday night in 1969 that Jim Whitted from Good News Baptist Church in Candler, North Carolina, called me and asked me if I could preach for them on Sunday morning. At that time, Good News Baptist Church did not have a pastor.

I agreed to preach. When I ended my sermon on Sunday morning, I turned it over to Jim, who was the moderator, and then I turned around and sat down in the choir. Jim, after a few comments, called on one of the ladies to pray. There were some godly women in that church that could pray heaven down. When they started praying, the Spirit of the Lord came down upon me and said to me, "This is where I want you." No one said anything after the service about me coming back and preaching.

Jim called me that evening and asked me if I could come back on Sunday night, to which I agreed. This went on for about six weeks, then, Lebo Murray, one of the pillars in the church, said to me, "We believe you are the one that God wants here" but said, "You never have announced your call to preach." (I had always been afraid of making a mistake, so I set my face to seek the Lord, and I got settled it was my calling). What I had done, was "Jack-legged" preaching, you might say. I had been preaching ever since I got saved. Brother Zeb McDaris would call on me to testify, and I would preach. My daddy-in-law, Rev. Bill House, had me to preach on different occasions for him. I had the opportunity to preach up and down the aisles of many churches in the drama. So, on a Saturday night Cottage Prayer meeting, I announced I was surrendering to preach the gospel of Jesus Christ until he comes.

But when Brother Lebo Murray said, "Are you called to preach or not?" I had to settle the matter. I didn't want to make a mistake. I began to pray, and the Lord said,

"This is what I want you to do." On the Sunday that they were voting on me at Good News Baptist, I was preaching a weekend meeting for Rev. James Wooten in Belmont, North Carolina at the Brown town Baptist Church. As I sat there behind the pulpit, waiting to preach, knowing that Good News Church was voting on me to become their pastor, I said "Lord, I don't know enough to preach three sermons a week." The Lord said, "I will give it to you." Do you know that in fifty-three years of preaching, God has kept His word. I remember when I was at Zion Hill, I walked out of the kitchen door and walked into my study, which was only a few steps between those two doors, and God gave me a sermon. Praise the Lord, hallelujah. God is faithful. My first sermon at Good News was "Go Forward."

In my fifty-three years of pastoring churches, I have accumulated a lot of sermons. I recall being at a church yard sale, and they had a filing cabinet for sale. I was talking to the assistant pastor. I told him I had several filing cabinets full of sermons, and I needed another filing cabinet. When the pastor came in, the assistant pastor told him it seemed to me, that he was totally shocked, that I had so many sermons that I had filled filing cabinets with them. No wonder some preachers only preach one sermon a week.

1st Church

Kuykendall Will Be Ordained

Leo Kuykendall will be ordained as a Baptist minister Wednesday night at Mt. Pisgah Baptist Church. He is a member of the Mt. Pisgah Church.

and will accept the pastoral of Good News Baptist Church.

The Rev. W. M. Belcher will deliver the ordination sermon, the Rev. Zeb McDaris, the charge; and the Rev. Walter Hare will present Mr. Kuykendall with a Bible. Other ministers participating in the service will be the Rev. Claude Surrett, the Rev. Van Greene and the Rev. Don Gasperson.

The Enka- Candler (N. C.) Record

THE REV. LEO KUYKENDALL has accepted a call as pastor to the Good News Baptist Church in Candler. He is married to the former Miss Carolyn House and they have two children, Otis Leo, Jr. and Sherry. He has been an active member of Mt. Pisgah Baptist Church.

**Good News Baptist Church
Candler, North Carolina**

On June 1, 1969, I became the pastor of Good News Baptist Church in Candler, North Carolina, where I pastored until March 31, 1974. I had some praying people at Good News, especially praying women. One night after coming out of the prayer room, some of the women slipped into a Sunday school room. The service had already begun, then; the ladies came out praising the Lord. Sister Reba Trull had a tremendous burden for her son, so they stayed and prayed for his salvation. They came out with victory. Her son, who had long hair (he said he wasn't coming to church), got saved in two weeks from their praying. He came to church and set on the second pew from the front with his hair cut and was saying amen to the preaching. God can change people. 2 Corinthians 5:17 says, "Therefore if any man be in Christ, he is a new creature: old things are passed away; behold, all things are new."

Mighty Men

David had his mighty men, and so have I had mighty men in every church that I have pastored. Every pastor must have his mighty men who stand with him to fight the battle against Satan. It is a must. I certainly can't name all the mighty men that God has given me in all three churches. Also, I've had some mighty women to be my helpers, but I only name a few.

At Good News Baptist Church, I had Brother Jim Whitted, Brother Jerry Young, Brother Lebo Murray, Brother Charlie Lance and Brother Bruce Murray. Of course, there were many others also. I had some of Godly women who could pray heaven down in Good News. They sure knew how to ring the prayer bells of heaven.

When I first went to Good News, Brother Lebo Murray made this statement after I became their pastor, "We need to pray for this preacher. The devil has never fought him like he will now." He was so right.

One night while at Good News, after the service was dismissed, a man gave me a blessing out. I thought to myself, *If that's the way you feel, I'll just resign right now.* I looked around, and everybody had already left. There was no one to resign to. The Lord taught me a great lesson. You don't act on impulses but impressions from the Lord. I didn't resign but stayed at Good News five years before the Lord called me to Zion Hill in Marion, North Carolina.

Good News did not have a deacon board. Remember, this was a newly organized church. They had Men's Meeting, where all the men of the church participated. Brother Lebo Murray was the moderator. I remember Lebo saying in one of their meetings, "We have got to get this boy off those telephone poles." I was still working at Southern Bell at that time. Of course, that is what the church did, and I have been a full-time pastor ever since!

We had some great women at Good News Baptist Church. Mrs. Murray, Mrs. Parham, and Mrs. Perry, along with other women, could pray with mighty power. One of them was sister Jackie Lance, who wrote the whole program for our VBS. She wrote it for every class. What ability and what blessings.

Sister Sophie Fender was very sensitive about babies crying in the service. If someone's baby was crying, and they did not take him or her to the nursery, she would go to them and say, "Let me take your baby to the nursery."

JoAnn Brooks was an unusual lady. After service, she would check all the windows to make sure they were shut and locked. Also, she would check the bathrooms. This was because we didn't have a custodian at that time. One Sunday, we had a seven-hour prayer after the morning service. We started at 12:00 pm and went till 7:00 pm. Of all the people who participated, JoAnn was the only one who prayed for seven hours without stopping.

JoAnn Brooks &Wanda Taylor
(she was our neighbor when growing up)

Tom Pinkerton has been a lifelong friend. He rode to work with me when I worked at Champion Paper. When I became the pastor of Good News Baptist Church, he came to hear me preach. In fact, everywhere that I have pastored, he came. When I came to Zion Baptist Church, we supported Tom as a building missionary. He was a carpenter by trade, so he used his talent on the mission field. Further, Tom has helped me in renting my little place that we left when we moved to Zion Hill in Marion, North Carolina.

Me with Missionary Tom Pinkerton & Carolyn

Tom made seven trips to Papua, New Guinea. He helped build five churches, a Bible school, and six missionary houses. Further, he went to Peru, where he built a school, a church, and a medical center. These structures will keep blessing folks for years to come.

Tom laughs all the time, which deceives a lot of people. They thought that he was a pushover. What they didn't know was when he said something, he means it. People have found it out with tough consequences.

Further, I have had a lot of folks give me books over the years. Brother Bruce Murray gave me the first book of Charles Spurgeon's sermons, the *Metropolitan Tabernacle Pulpit*. Spurgeon has been called the "Prince of Preachers." It was the first volume off the press. After that, I bought them one by one as they were printed. There are sixty-three volumes. What a gift Brother Bruce gave me.

During my ministry, I have had a lot of great preachers preach revivals for me. At Good News Baptist, I had Rev. Bill Hensley, Dr. Ken Love of Wytheville, Virginia, Rev. Charles Worley, Rev. Ray Long, Dr. Harold Sightler, the pastor of Tabernacle Baptist Church in Greenville, South Carolina, Dr. Curtis McCarley, the pastor of Balfour Baptist Church in Balfour, North Carolina—Brother Curtis had an accident with a dump truck that took his life at the age of forty-three—Rev. Bob Wardlaw from Georgia, and Dr. Russel Rice, from Greenville, South Carolina. All of these men were great preachers and mighty men of God.

One of the preachers that I asked to preach a revival for us was Rev. Kenneth Faulkenbury. It was in the month of February when the weather can be cold and snowy, especially in that month. On Thursday night, he didn't show up. I certainly was not prepared to preach, but I made a stab at it. The reason he didn't show up was because he was driving from Marion, North Carolina to Candler, North Carolina. By the way, he was the pastor of Zion Hill Baptist Church at that time. When he got to Black Mountain, there was ice all over the place. He thought it would be that way all the way to Candler. But what he didn't know was that there was not a bit of ice at our church in Candler. The lesson here is to always be prepared.

The morning that I resigned at Good News Baptist, after I read the Scripture that I was going to preach on, I said, "Let us pray." I knelt down behind the pulpit, but I could not say a word. I was so filled with emotion over leaving that I could not utter one word. Not one word would come out. My daddy-in-law, Rev. Bill House, was there that morning. He recognized my condition, and he started praying. Resigning from a church is not easy, especially if you love your people.

My Call to Zion Hill

The Old Zion Hill Baptist Church

While I was pastor of Good News Baptist, a pulpit committee from Zion Hill Baptist Church came to hear me preach. So I preached a weekend revival for them. After I preached that Sunday morning, everyone came around to shake hands with me. George Marlowe leaned over and asked me, "Are you a Baptist?" I said, "Yes." And he said, "Good." I guess the way I preached he thought I might be a Pentecostal preacher. Brother George passed away on January 23, 1978, at the age of eighty-one, and his wife Grace passed away three months later, on April 15, 1978, at the age of seventy-seven. George and his wife Grace were great souls. After everyone came around, the pulpit committee asked if they could vote on me. I said, "Yes." On the Sunday that they voted on me, Brother Loren Laney called me. He said, "The majority voted for you." I asked for the numbers. He didn't want to tell me. I got two-thirds of the vote. One-third voted against me. Zion Hill was a divided church on doctrines. Some believed in the premillennial doctrine and some in the amillennial doctrine. Brother Laney said, "We want to come and talk to you before you give your answer," so I agreed. When I hung up the phone, I thought a man would be a fool to take a church with one-third of the people against him, so I made up my mind to say no to them. That Sunday evening, the pulpit committee came to talk to me. Loren said, "You've got to understand the nature of the church—part premillennial and part amillennial." He said, "If it had been a Dr. Percy Ray, a Dr. Harold Sightler, or Dr. J. Harold Smith, it would have been the same vote." These were great preachers. I told them, "I would be a fool to take a church with that vote." They said, "Will you pray about it?" I thought it wouldn't hurt to pray, so I agreed.

Loren & Wilma Laney

The premillennial belief is that the next thing on God's time calendar is the rapture of the church. The transformation of the living saints and the resurrection of the dead saints, and both will be raptured to heaven together. Then there will be seven years of tribulation called the 1. great tribulation, 2. the day of the Lord, and 3. the time of Jacob's trouble. The antichrist will demand worship and make war on the Jewish people. Then, after the seven years of tribulations, Jesus will descend from heaven with all the saints and set up His kingdom and reign for a 1000 years, ruling from Jerusalem.

The amillennial belief is that when Jesus comes, there will be a general resurrection of the saved and sinners and a general judgment. There will not be a 1,000-year reign of Christ on earth. These are the two views of the coming of the Lord.

I took several weeks to give them an answer. I guess they thought I would never give them an answer. One day, as I was praying, I looked up at a plaque on our mirror; it was Joshua 1:9, "Have not I commanded thee? Be strong and of a good courage; be not afraid, neither be thou dismayed: for the Lord thy God is with thee withersoever thou goest." God said, "That is your answer." So, I went to Zion Hill Baptist Church with that promise. I was there almost twenty years. Every time it looked like I was going down, I claimed that verse again. God keeps his promises. You can certainly depend on that. I had a great ministry at Zion Hill.

Before I went to Zion Hill, I talked to a former pastor, Rev. Floyd Beaver. I asked him about Zion Hill. He said, "One thing about that church, if the devil was preaching, they would go to church." I said, "That's my kind of church." Also, I had sat under Rev. Bill Belcher at Mt. Pisgah Baptist Church, who also was a former pastor of Zion Hill. In some of his sermons, he would mention Zion Hill. I never dreamed that one day I would pastor that church. Rev. Belcher passed away on January 5, 2004, at the age of eighty-nine.

INTRODUCING
The Rev. O.L. Kuykendall
Family of
Zion Hill Baptist Church

Family pictured left to right are: Tammy, Carolyn, Odie, Rev. Kuykendall, Sherry.

Rev. O.L. Kuykendall began his pastorate at the Zion Hill Baptist Church, Marion, N.C. in April, 1974. Before assuming his duties at the Zion Hill Baptist Church he was pastor of Good News Baptist Church, Candler, N.C.

He attended Fruitland Bible Institute for two years and is a 1974 graduate of Tabernacle Bible Institute, Greenville, South Carolina, with a Bachelor of Theology degree.

He is presently enrolled in Gardner Webb College, Boiling Springs, North Carolina.

The Zion Hill Baptist Church radio broadcast, "The Bible Hour", may be heard each Sunday morning on WWNC, 570 on your radio dial, from 7:30 A.M. until 8:00 A.M. & also on WAGI FM STATION, GAFNEY, S.C. each Sunday night from 7:00 P.M until 7:30 P.M.

Schedule of services at the Zion Hill Baptist Church are as follows:

Sunday School	9:45 a.m.
Worship Service	11:00 a.m.
Training Union	6:30 p.m.
Sunday Evening Service	7:30 p.m.
Wednesday Nite Service	7:30 p.m.
Special Singing each Second Saturday night in each month	7:30 p.m.

After I accepted the call to Zion Hill Baptist Church in Marion, North Carolina. I was blessed to be their pastor until December 7, 1993 (twenty years, lacking four months). My first sermon at Zion Hill was "How Good Is Your Vision?"

At Zion Hill, I had some mighty men, such as Brother John Trent and his family. We ate my first meal with him and his family and our last meal with his wife, Mrs. Thelma Trent, because John had gone on to heaven on August 15, 1991. When they told Austin Ramsey, his grandson, that he had gone on to heaven, he said, "Let's go see him." John was one of my deacons and also one of my best friends. He stood with his pastor.

John & Thelma Trent with me in
Lexington, Kentucky

Rev. Keith Jamison & me

After becoming Zion Hill's pastor, I would sometimes drive a van to pick up kids for church. I picked up one young boy named Keith Jamison. Today, Rev. Keith Jamison pastors the Living Waters Tabernacle. My grandson, Nick, has gone there off and on. Rev Jamison told Nick that, "Your granddad took me to church and witnessed to me, and I got saved, and now I'm witnessing to his grandson." God saved him and called him to preach, and now he is a pastor. Rev Keith, before he became a pastor, played the piano and had a group of singers called the "Fortresses," and they sang for different churches. God's ways are mysterious and wonderous to behold! Job 9:10 says the Lord "doeth great things past finding out; yea, wonders without numbers."

One Sunday evening, we visited Denise and Dennis Beam, who lived right below Zion Hill Baptist Church. Denise was Loren Laney's daughter of who was the moderator of the pulpit committee. Denise was the organist at Zion Hill for many years. They were telling us that they couldn't have children, but they had tried. I said, "Let's ask the Lord about it," so we prayed and asked the Lord to give them children. It wasn't long until they were expecting a baby. It turned out that they had two girls and a boy. God does answer prayers.

Front row: Dennis & Denise Beam
Back row: Brandi, Kristi,
& Justin Beam

Fred & Mae Wright

The Wright family, Fred and Mae and James and Nan, fed us many Sundays. Fred and James were brothers, and they married sisters, Mae and Nan. James and Nan's daughter Sylvia and Fred and Mae's daughter Linda looked a lot alike. Well, they should have since they were "double first cousins." These two brothers were go-getters. They would get on each end of a log with chainsaws and work like termites cutting it up. James Wright passed away on August 17, 1996, at the age of seventy-seven. His wife Nan passed away on February 6, 2014, at the age of ninety-three. Fred Wright passed away on May 29, 2015, at the age of ninety-two. Fred's wife Mae passed away May 29, 2022 at the age of 98 years old.

James & Nan Wright

Front row: Paul & Frances Baker
Back row: Ivan & Nathan Baker

Also, Brother Paul Baker and his wife Francis were great friends and helpers. I had preached a weekend meeting at Zion Hill before I became the pastor. I did not know that Brother Paul Baker got saved in that meeting until many years later when I was at Zion in Gastonia. When Paul came and spoke as a Gideon at Zion in his speaking, he said he got saved in that meeting. Paul and Frances gave me a set of J. Vernon McGee's "Through the Bible" commentaries. I have used them almost on a weekly basis. What a blessing!

Winston Worley had a lot to do with my going to Zion Hill church. Brother Winston listened to my radio broadcast all the time. When they were looking for a pastor, Winston told the pulpit committee that they needed to go listen to Leo Kuykendall. Well, the rest is history. But there is something else that I have to say about Brother Winston. On every birthday that I had while at Zion Hill, Brother Winston gave me a pair of Mason shoes. What a gift. He kept me "shod" with excellent shoes. Winston passed away on September 25, 2001, at the age of eighty-eight.

Winston & Gladys Worley

I mentioned Brother Carl Hensley earlier. He was one of my mighty men at Zion Hill. He always sat on the front pew and gave those amens at the preaching. He went with me on visitation on Thursday night and Saturdays. Carl couldn't read, but he was thrilled with Revelation 1:3, where it said, "Blessed is he that readeth, and they that hear the words of this prophecy . . ." He said, "That included me." Every Saturday morning, Brother Carl rolled up to the parsonage and blew his horn. He had already been to the flea market and brought us a bag of tomatoes.

Carl Hensley in front of the Zion Hill pulpit

In one of my sermons, as I was preaching on Jesus dying for us, I said, "Who would you die for? Probably your family. But who else would you die for?" After that, as Brother Carl and I were out on visitation, he said, "Preacher, I would die for you." To me, that was overwhelming. Then on another occasion, he told me the same thing again. That is what is called "Christian love." Brother Carl passed away on October 21, 1989, at the age of eighty. His wife Olive passed away on December 27, 1982, at the age of seventy-one.

I met Dr. John Phillips at Faith Baptist Camp, where he had preached. I asked him about preaching a revival for me. I was at Zion Hill Baptist in Marion at that time. He said, "I am not an evangelist." I said, "I know it, but I still want you to come anyway." I scheduled him to come the last four days of the year. I enjoyed his preaching and also the fellowship that we had together. He could not believe that I preached three sermons a week and sometimes four times a week because he spent so much time on just one of his sermons. He only preached one sermon a week. Of course, his sermons were a lot better than mine. He had a lot of his sermons in books. He could not understand preachers using his sermons. I said to him, "You have them in print? Of course, preachers will use them." Dr. John was a sweet man. I thank God that I was able to have him in revival. He authored more than fifty books. He died on July 25, 2010, at the age of eighty-three.

Dr. John Phillips

While Dr. John Phillips was with me in a revival meeting, I mentioned that I did not have a secretary, and then he said, "Preacher, you need a secretary." After that, Sister Betty Payne was voted in as my first secretary. She was the one who started out with me on my journey with the book that turned out to be *The God of the Bible* in two volumes. Sister Betty was a preacher's friend. She sure took up for me many times. She was married to Dillard Payne who was one of my Deacons. Their daughter, Bobbie Kay became very close to us. In fact, Carolyn calls her "My little red-headed step daughter." She calls Carolyn "Mother" and me "Pops." She has stayed in contact with Carolyn through the years. Dillard passed away April 28, 2018, at the age of ninety. His wife Betty passed away April 8, 1997, at the age of sixty-four.

My first secretary, Betty Payne & husband Dillard

One dear brother, who was my right-hand man for about eighteen years, listened to some gossip and turned against me. The devil will do it to a preacher if he can. He would sit in the front seat and point his finger at me to irritate me. People thought he was backing me because that is what he had always done up until that time. I tried to talk with him, but he would never make things right. After I left Zion Hill, a tragedy happened to that brother. He was caught in a machine that severed his head and threw it against the wall of the machine shop, where he worked at. It took four hours to get him out of the machine. I sure was so sorry about it because he had been one of my mighty men for those eighteen years. The Bible says in 1 Chronicles 16:22 and Psalm 105:15, "Touch not mine anointed, and do my prophets no harm." Remember, be careful what you do in the house of God. He did call and apologized for his actions before he died. He was only fifty-seven years old when he died.

Another instance of this I want to mention. A lady was driving down the road, and it was dark, a tractor and trailer was backing across the road. The trailer had no lights on, and she ran under the trailer and would have been decapitated if she had not ducked. When I visited her at the hospital, she said, "I'm sorry." She had been spreading lies about me. Be careful what you do to God's man.

Zion Hill was a great church; they had singing schools every two or three years. Thus, they had a great choir and great singers. Burder Worley was the choir leader for many years. He passed away on May 13, 2007, at the age of eighty-nine. His wife Edith passed away on June 1, 2010, at the age of eighty-seven.

Burder & Edith Worley

The Worley Family, the Sprinkle Family, the Laney Family, the Epley Family, and the Wright Family were big families in Zion Hill. Some have stayed in contact with us over the years. The Trent Family, Shirley Pitman, the Ramsey Family, Carolyn Ledford, who made the best fudge candy you have ever put in your mouth, John & Debbie Carver, Mary Reed, Judy Kuykendall, whose husband Buddy Kuykendall was a third or fourth cousin, and, of course, others. What a great church, what great people! They were long life people. I preached the funeral of four people who were over a 100 years old.

JB, Jo & Joanne Epley

John & Thelma Trent

Shirley Pittman

Carolyn Ledford

John & Debbie Carver

Bobby, Mary & Barbara Reed

Wayne & Velva Ramsey

While at Zion Hill, one of the girls in the church was to be married to a boy in Dr. Charles Stanley's church, the First Baptist Church, in Atlanta, Georgia. The wedding was to be on a Saturday. I got someone to preach for me on Sunday so that Carolyn and I could go to the wedding and stay to hear Dr. Stanley preach on Sunday. That Sunday, the service turned out to be a different type of service. Someone had leaked the church's plans to build a new church to one of the newspapers in Atlanta, Georgia. The facts that were printed were wrong. So, that Sunday was dedicated to setting the facts straight. Dr. Stanley said, "You don't need to take notes. He went on to say that we were not going to vote on anything. "A pamphlet will be given to you as you go out. Go home and read it, then come back tonight and ask any questions that you may have." Slides were shown going all the way back to the first church, showing the different churches that had been built through the years. It was a tremendous presentation.

Dr. Charles Stanley

After the slide presentation, Dr. Stanley talked about raising the money. We sat on the third pew from the front. A lady jumped up about two pews behind us and said, "Dr. Stanley, I can tell you how to get the money." Dr. Stanley said, "Sit down, you are out of order." She kept on, "Dr. Stanley, I can tell you how to get the money, and you will not have to borrow it." Dr. Stanley said, "Sit down, you are out of order." She kept on, so Dr. Stanley said, "Take her out." As the ushers were rushing her out, she began screaming, "You think I'm crazy, you think I'm crazy." I thought it was a crazy thing she did to interrupt a church service full of people while Dr. Stanley was talking. Such a display like that was unnerving to everyone. I would say that most of the congregation did think she was crazy.

While at Zion Hill, we were able to build a 10,000-square-foot Sunday school building. Later, we built a new church that would seat 800 people. The first floor seated 530, the choir seated 70, and the balcony seated 200. When I was building the new church at Zion Hill, I had some encouragers and some discouragers. Some of my preacher friends that I looked up to, when they saw the hull of the church, said, "Leo, you have built too big." That brought a dark cloud over me. I sure could not change anything because the cement floor was poured, and the church had been framed in. I said, "Lord, I don't want to do anything wrong or against your will." But then there were encouragers. Rev. Dr. Ralph Sexton Sr. of Trinity Baptist Church in Asheville, North Carolina, came by, and I told him what some had said. He replied, "Build it until it sticks out over the road because it was built on a hill, and build the steeple up to heaven." What an encouragement that was! Dr. Sexton Sr. passed away on January 13, 2004, at the age of eighty-four. Still further, I stopped by Rev. Dr. Jimmy Robbins, who pastored Mountain View Baptist Church in Cowpens, South Carolina. I was telling him about building a new church. He said, "Make it beautiful; it is the house of God, so make it beautiful." And that is what we did. Many people that went through the new church said it was the most beautiful church they had ever seen. To God be the glory! Dr. Robbins preached a revival for us at Zion Hill. He personally helped me more than any other preacher that I ever had in revival. Dr. Robbins, known as the "Son of Thunder," passed away on January 9, 2010, at the age of seventy-eight.

Rev. Jim Robbins
"Son of Thunder"

When we built Zion Hill, I said, "I don't want any steps. It is a sin to have steps around a church." The reason I came to that conclusion is that I went to a funeral at another church, and when I got there, the church was full. I had to stand in the foyer. This foyer had once been the porch of that church. They had enclosed it and made it part of the church. However, they left a step from the main church to the old porch. I stood there and watched the people exit, and half the people stumbled when they came to that step. It might not be a sin to put steps around a church, but they certainly will become stumbling blocks. Thus, when we built Zion Hill, there is only one step in front of the porch. The reason we put one seven-inch step was because the driveway went in front of the church, and we didn't want someone to knock the columns down on the porch. There are no steps all the way around the church. No one had an excuse that they couldn't get in the church because of steps, because there were no steps.

Carolyn & Me
Zion Hill Parking Lot

New Zion Hill Baptist Church – Arial View – 1036 Zion Hill Rd,
Marion, North Carolina

God is still a God of miracles. Some said, "You will never get the money to build," and we did. Some said, "You will never get it paid for. Our grandkids will be paying on it." But by the help of God, we paid it off in nine years and burned the note before I left.

There is another miracle I experienced while pouring the sidewalks at Zion Hill. It was on a Saturday, close to 12:00 pm, when the cement plant closed down, the pour was right on the corner. It was a big pour. When the cement was dumped out of the cement truck, the cement was just a little dab. The concrete finisher, who had been pouring concrete for years, said, "That's not near enough, preacher." I said, "Lord, let it be enough." He said it too late to pray preacher, of course it was not I said to the truck driver, "Crank that cement mixer back up." The driver did, but none came out. They started spreading the cement out, and would you believe, there was not a spoonful less, not a spoonful over. It filled that corner perfectly. In the New Testament, Jesus multiplied fish and bread. That day, God multiplied cement. I saw a miracle right before my eyes!

Carolyn, me, & Sherry
In front of and in the parking lot of the New Zion Hill Baptist Church

A funny thing happened when we built the new church at Zion Hill. When the contractor got the new building finished, we tore the old church down. The well for the church was right beside the old church. When the old church was gone, then the well was in the middle of the parking lot. One of the members came up to see the new church, and some of the men where there working. That member said, "How did the well get out there in the middle of the parking lot?" One of the men working said, "We moved it." The member stood there a minute, and then he said, "Oh, you didn't." It took a minute for him to realize what had happened.

Me at the new Zion Hill pulpit
I liked that pulpit more than any pulpit I have ever stood behind.

Right after we dedicated the new church, Lynn Green brought his home video camera and was recording a special event. I saw what he was doing and thought, *We need a video camera to video the preaching services.* Zion Hill purchased a video camera, and we went on a leased TV channel, ACCN in Asheville, North Carolina for a time. Steve "Burgie" Burleson, who ran that particular channel, did the editing as we did not have editing equipment. He said he was watching the screen and, all of a sudden, I ran out of the picture, and then I came back. He was a dear and encouraging brother. I learned that he passed away on October 12, 2015, at the age of sixty-six. It makes me sad that he is gone.

Steve "Burgie" Burleson

After we built the new church at Zion Hill, we didn't have any good pictures of the church to put on our letterhead and use for the newspaper ads. One reason why we couldn't get any good pictures was because there were power lines and telephone lines in the picture, so Brother Paul Baker paid for the rental of a helicopter to fly from Asheville, North Carolina, to Marion, North Carolina, to take pictures of the church. The pilot let me ride with him and a girl that he had to take the picture. He took the door off and let her hang outside of the helicopter to take the pictures. She was in a harness. He flew around the church several times, getting some great pictures. It was a thrill for me to get that view from the air.

New Zion Hill Baptist Church

While at Zion Hill in Marion, North Carolina, I had several great preachers to preach revivals. Rev. Richard Horney preached the first revival in the new church. I still remember some of the things he preached. I preached at a "Watch Night Service" for Brother Richard at Bible Way Baptist in Boone, North Carolina. I also preached a revival for him in Pequoson, Virginia. While I was with him, Brother Richard took me to different tourist sites, The William & Mary College, Langley Air Force Base, and a wind tunnel. He had a lot of service people in his church there. One of the men took me out to the base, and I got to climb up and look into the cockpit of an F-15 fighter jet. One thing shocked me. I saw no padding of any kind in the cockpit. Also, I got to see the heat-seeking missiles up close. Before Brother Richard took the assistant pastor's position at Baptist Tabernacle, he came to our church several times. He was a great man, a great preacher, and a great soul winner, who had a great voice, who left a great legacy. Rev. Horney passed away on June 5, 2009, at the age of sixty-five.

Rev. Richard Horney Jr.

Dr. Curtis Barbery

Also, Dr. Jimmy Robbins, Rev. Sammy Allen, "The walking Bible," from Resaca, Georgia, Rev. Carl Lackey of White Plains Baptist Church in Mt. Airy, North Carolina, and Dr. Curtis Barbery. Dr. Curtis preached one of the greatest sermons I had ever heard on "David's Mighty Men." Rev. Bob Wardlaw, DD, from Atlanta, Georgia, Rev. Charles Worley, Dr. Ed Ballew, founder of Rock of Ages Prison Ministry in Cleveland, Tennessee, Dr. Stinnett Ballew of Resaca, Georgia, and Dr. Percy Ray; great men, great preachers, with great anointing. Many of the sermons of these men can be heard on the internet.

Rev. Bob Wardlaw passed away on December 23, 2017, at the age of eighty-one, one of the greatest preachers I ever heard preach. Rev. Carl Lackey passed away on June 13, 1993, at the age of seventy-eight. Dr. Ed Ballew passed away on November 18, 2010, at the age of eighty-six. Dr. Stinnett Ballew passed away on May 31, 2019, at the age of seventy-seven. What a loss for us, but what a joy up in heaven when these soldiers went home to be with Jesus. Revelation 14:13 says, "And I heard a voice from heaven saying unto me, Write, Blessed are the dead which die in the Lord from henceforth: Yea, saith the Spirit, that they may rest from their labours; and their works do follow them."

Rev. Bob Wardlaw

Rev. Carl Lackey

Dr. Ed Ballew   Dr. Stinnett Ballew

The preachers that came to preach revivals for me were never left in a motel by themselves. I would pick them up around 10:00 am, and we would go places together and a have a time of fellowship.

When I was at Zion Hill in Marion, North Carolina, I preached a lot of revivals. Rev. Ken Burleson, pastor of Faith Baptist Church, began what he called "A One Night Jubilee," and then later, he called it "A One Night Revival." It was a privilege to be one of the preachers for thirty-one years. Usually, the first preacher will be Dr. Lewis Grant from Asheville, North Carolina, then Rev. Jimmy Upton of Marion, North Carolina, and then me. For the last three years, Dr. Bob McCurry has been added to the list. All of these men are great preachers.

Rev. Ken Burleson   Dr. Bob McCurry & Me
Faith Baptist Church

I had heard of Dr. Percy Ray many times before I ever met him. What a powerful preacher he was. Dr. Percy was preaching a revival at Maple Grove Baptist Church in the Stamey Cove, which was a few miles out of Canton, North Carolina. So, I went to hear Dr. Percy. When I saw him, I thought to myself, *That fellow can't preach.* He looked like an Episcopalian to me with a black suit on. But it didn't take me long to change my mind when he started preaching. He titled his message "Blood on a Rock and Scum in the Pot." That was a powerful sermon. That was the first of many sermons that I would hear him preach over the years. You can listen to Dr. Percy Ray's sermons on www.freegospelpreaching.com by selecting "speakers," and on www. campzion1949.org, then select "Dr. Percy Ray" on the lefthand side.

Dr. Percy Ray

I remember different experiences I had with Dr. Percy Ray. He was with me in several revivals during those times. While he was with me one time in revival, I was to preach in a church in Cherokee, North Carolina. I picked up Dr. Ray and tried to get him to preach instead of me. He said, "No, they are expecting you to preach." After the service was over, and we were headed home, he said, "You had the attention of those Indians. They were listening to you."

Another time, I took Dr. Ray up on the Blue Ridge Parkway. We stopped at an overlook. We got out and enjoyed the beautiful view of the mountains. I turned and finally got in the car. Dr. Ray stood there like a soldier at attention. Then after a while, he turned and walked over to the edge of pavement and was looking at the rock cliff on the other side of the road. Then he came and got in the car and said, "God is talking to me up here on these mountains."

Dr. Percy was a strong man. I took him all the way to "Bush Brother's Beans" near Sevierville, Tennessee; that is where he bought a lot of his canned vegetables for Camp Zion. It probably was 120 miles one way, and he had to preach that night. Most preachers would have been exhausted and unable to preach, but not Dr. Percy.

Dining Hall at Camp Zion in Myrtle, Mississippi

Another time, Dr. Percy was to preach a revival for me, and I drove to Kings Mountain, North Carolina, from Zion Hill in Marion, North Carolina, to pick up Dr. Percy. He had been preaching for another pastor, so we met halfway. Odie was with me and was about thirteen years old. Dr. Percy told us a lot of his experiences. Odie and I thoroughly enjoyed listening to those stories. In one of those meetings that Dr Percy preached for me, he stayed with us at the parsonage. Dr. Percy always loved to eat soup in the outset of his meals. After Dr. Percy left to go home, he left a note pinned to his pillow that read, "Thanks, Mrs. Kuykendall, for everything. You are an angel." Carolyn had washed his shirts, and he was so appreciative. Carolyn wishes to this day that she had kept that note. It meant so much to her.

One time, I was at Camp Zion. Dr. Percy said, "Ten of you pastors come up here and preach five minutes each." This he did every conference that he had. I wasn't going up, but some of my members encouraged me to go on up. So I finally went, but I was scared because I had never preached to that many people, let alone all the preachers that were there. The tabernacle seated almost 2,000. But one thing that I discovered was that it is easier to preach to a big crowd than a small one. It was a great experience.

Dr. Percy Ray had a great burden for America. It was a time of rebellion, protesting, and violence during the 1960s and 1970s. Dr. Percy called on the preachers and others who came to Camp Zion to pray. One year, he had someone pray for revival in America every day in the year. Another year, he had different churches in each state go to the capital grounds in their state and pray for America on a specific day at an appointed hour. Later, J. Edgar Hoover, head of the FBI, told Dr. Percy, "Had it not been for you (Dr. Percy) and Camp Zion praying, the Communists would have taken over America." Thank God for Dr. Percy Ray and Camp Zion during a time such as that (Esther 4:13–14). The same thing is taking place today. It is time for God's people to fast and pray for America. Dr. Percy Ray passed away on April 11, 1991, at the age of eighty.

Dr. Percy Ray
This is the Percy I remember.

It is time again for God's people to pray again for revival in America, for these are turbulent times. The Marxists are trying to take over America. Again, they are doing what the Marxists did in other countries they took over, Russia, China, North Korea, and Venezuela. An immigrant from Venezuela said that what they are doing in America by tearing down statues, renaming streets, and institutions is exactly what they did in the takeover of Venezuela. America needs to wake up before it is too late.

While pastoring Zion Hill, we took the young people to Camp Zion in Myrtle, Mississippi. We had a full busload. I remember standing in front of the bus, talking to the driver, Brother Gary Brown. All of a sudden, the noise of the motor changed. I said to Brother Gary, "Wonder what caused that motor noise to change?" All of a sudden, bang! And the bus lost power. The motor had thrown a rod. We were on I-40 in Jackson, Tennessee. Brother Gary and I walked to a service station to use a telephone. There were other adults on the bus who stayed with the kids. These were the days before cell phones. I called Dr. Percy Ray and told him what had happened. He said he would send a bus to pick us up. In the meantime, we had the bus pulled to a garage. We waited quite a while on the bus to come and get us. A bus from Peoria, Illinois, came and took us to Camp Zion. When we got there, Dr. Percy told me he had found another motor to put in the bus close by. Further, he said he would get the bus towed from Jackson, Tennessee, to Myrtle, Mississippi, and have the motor put in by the time the conference would be over. That was a scary time being broken down on the side of the interstate that far away from home with a busload of kids. The church back home said, "Anything you have to do, do it." Also, Dr. Percy Ray took hold of the situation and took care of it. We had a better bus when we left the camp than when we came down. But the men who exchanged the motors got the wires messed up. We had to stop in Jackson, Tennessee, and get the wires straightened out. The youth had a great time at Camp Zion.

Zion Hill Sunday school revival, August 1987
Mr. Sunday School, Rev. Leon Kilbreth spoke.
He is standing in the front row.

View showing balcony during Sunday school revival at Zion Hill

Left to right, Rev. Allen McKinney, Leon Kilbreth (Mr. Sunday School), and me

Another unusual thing that happened was when I married a couple at Zion Hill. I was observing the couple while the wedding ceremony was taking place. I wondered if they even loved each other. They did not show any emotion of love. So it made me wonder. While the reception was taking place, I wanted to ask them who they wanted to sign the marriage certificate for witnesses. I could not find them in the room where the reception was taking place. So, I went back in the church, and there they were, all hugged up, kissing each other. They had got away from the crowd to show their love for each other. I sure was glad to see that.

Missionary Kenneth Cates

One of the greatest missionaries I ever met was Brother Kenneth Cates from Burlington, North Carolina. He was a missionary to Brazil. Zion Hill supported him before I became the pastor. It was on a Sunday evening that he came to be with us to do his presentation. When he came to the parsonage, before service, he seemed so bashful. He could hardly look me in the eyes. I wondered what kind of a missionary that he was. When he got up to preach that night, that question disappeared. His theme was "Can God do today what He did in the days of Abraham?" Affirming that God could, all through his message. He related his call to be a missionary, his trip to Baltimore, Maryland, to get a visa, his trip to Brazil, and how the devil tried to discourage him.

He sat down outside the office, where he was to get his visa. He was overwhelmed.

He said, "When you are in trouble, the Lord will be with you." When he went in and got his visa, they stamped it as a permanent visa that even other main line missionaries could never get.

Brother Cates landed 1200 miles from where he planned to go in Brazil. He didn't know the language. He walked down the street, looking for English words on signs. But he didn't see any. He was getting hungry, and then he saw one of those buggies that had some kind of Brazilian food. He saw the money that others were using, and he saw he had some. So, he joined the crowd with the money in hand. The money was taken, and the food (something like a hot dog) was put in his hand. He finally got to the town where he was going. He was on the fourth floor of a hotel and looked out at the city. That night, he knew no one and could not speak the language, and he said the devil told him to jump out of the window and kill himself. But he said, "When you are in trouble, the Lord will be with you." That was a phrase that he used over and over. He chose to live with a family to learn the language and their culture and customs instead of going to language school. He stayed with this family for seven months.

One night, he was going up the Amazon River with a native guide, and a wave hit the boat, and he fell overboard. He tried to swim and catch the boat, but he couldn't. His partner was deaf and mute, so he could not hear Brother Kenneth crying for help. He said he just began to float because he was exhausted, and that there were piranha fish, the kind of fish that can kill you in just a few minutes. He said, "Lord, is this your will for me to die before I get to the place that you want me to serve?" "But when you are in trouble, the Lord will be with you." The deaf boy missed Brother Kenneth and turned the boat around and headed back down the river. He could not speak, so he could not yell for Brother Kenneth, so he used a lantern that he had, looking for Brother Kenneth. He could not see him, but Brother Kenneth saw him and swam to the boat and climbed back on board. Brother Kenneth established thirteen churches in Brazil in his forty years as a missionary. Yes, "When you are in trouble, the Lord will be with you." Kenneth Cates passed away on January 4, 2011, at the age of seventy-one.

Zion Baptist Church

Along about the time that Zion Baptist was interested in me as their pastor, Maple Ridge Baptist in Candler, North Carolina, asked me to come and preach a trial sermon there. The pulpit committee at Maple Ridge only had one question, "How much do you make?" Zion Hill was a big church, and I was the pastor at that time. When I preached the trial sermon and left to go home, I knew and Carolyn knew God did not want me at Maple Ridge at that time. I would have loved to have been their pastor. That would have meant moving back to our home, but it was not God's will. Maple Ridge is the home church of the "Primitives." Maple Ridge Baptist Church bought some land just above my house on Medford Branch Road and built a new church. Their first service was on Sunday, August 18, 2019, at their new location.

1995 photo of Zion Baptist Church, 2437 Propst Street, Gastonia, North Carolina

The chain of events that led me to be the pastor of Zion Baptist in Gastonia, North Carolina was that Rev. Kenneth Spirlin and I were good friends. We had known each other for thirty years. Rev. Kenneth and Kaywood Hale were fishing buddies. Brother Kaywood was on the pulpit committee for Zion Baptist, who was searching for a new pastor. Brother Johnny Mayes, Brother Lemuel Whisnant, Brother Clyde Wiggins, Brother Kenny Williams, and Brother Travis Ruffin were all on the pulpit committee. Rev. Spirlin knew that Zion was looking for a pastor. He told Kaywood that they needed to hear Rev. Kuykendall at Zion Hill preach. So, the pulpit committee came and heard me preach. Then I preached a weekend revival for Zion. A vote was taken, and so I have been the pastor at Zion since December 12, 1993. My first sermon at Zion Baptist was "Can God?" Most people will remember the first sermon that any pastor preaches.

I always said, "Preach the roughest sermon you have in a trial sermon. If they can take that, they can take anything else you preach." All may not agree with my thoughts on this, but that is all right.

When the pulpit committee from Zion Baptist came to hear me preach, they asked 10,000 questions, it seemed. I didn't know if I was good enough to be their pastor. It was because of their experience with their former pastor. Of course, they called me, and I went. As the Scripture says in Psalm 99:2, "The Lord is Great in Zion," and that has certainly been true. We have seen God answer a lot of prayers. He has touched and changed a lot of lives. We started a bus ministry, which has continued until this day. At one time, we had eight buses running. That is not many compared to some bigger churches.

Me in the Pulpit of Zion Baptist

Our First Bus

Billboard at corner of Hwy 321 South & Hudson Blvd

Zion Baptist Church of South Gastonia Has Called A New Pastor REV. LEO KUYKENDALL from Marion, N.C. along with his wife, CAROLYN

Rev. Kuykendall is the former pastor of the Zion Hill Baptist Church of Marion, N.C. where he has pastored for almost 20 years. He has maintained the "Bible Hour Radio Ministry" presently heard over 5 stations for 23 years.

He is a graduate of Tabernacle Baptist Bible Institute of Greenville, S.C. and Gardner-Webb College of Boiling Springs, N.C.

He will assume his role as the pastor of Zion Baptist Church Sunday, the 12th of December. We here at Zion Baptist Church extend to you and yours an invitation to come and worship with us. As Moses said in Numbers 10:29 "Come thou with us and we will do thee good."

Our church is located on Propst street two blocks off 321 South and Neal Hawkins Road.

After moving to Zion Baptist in Gastonia, I started broadcasting a TV program on Public Access Channel. Then we went to Charter Cable, and finally WKHY Channel 14 out of Hickory, North Carolina, which broadcasts on Spectrum, Charter Cable, Direct TV, Dish Network, and Comporium Cable. "The Bible Hour" still broadcasts every Wednesday night from 9:00 pm to 10:00 pm.

In all the churches that I have pastored, I loved the people. Yes, I have had people that left me for one reason or another, just as they left Jesus (John 6:65–66), just as they left Paul the apostle (Acts 15:37–39, 2 Timothy 4:10). If they left Jesus, the Son of God, and Paul the apostle, who am I to think that some will not leave me? I never have enjoyed seeing people leave, even if they have caused me trouble. I feel like I have failed in not reaching them with reconciliation.

I've met some interesting people along the way. One Sunday morning, we had a couple visit at Zion. When shaking hands at the door, I asked the husband about himself. He said he was from Israel, so I thought he was probably Jewish. After visiting them later at their home, he told me he was Assyrian. His family was living in Israel. Further, he told me there were only 4,000 Assyrians in the world. Of the seven kingdoms represented by the seven heads in Revelation 17, Assyria is the only one that is not in existence today. Could that be the one talked about in Revelation 13:3? "And I saw one of his heads as it were wounded to death; and his deadly wound was healed."

I insert these instances in so that many will take warning of how they ought to behave in the house of God. On a Sunday evening service, one of the deacons said, "Pastor, we need to have a deacon's meeting; we've got some trouble." We met, and he said that one of the members had gone to a lawyer and wanted to padlock the church and freeze our assets. The reason for this was we had voted to buy some property to build a new church in the future. This member was against it and went to a lawyer. The lawyer told him that he had never done anything like that before. The lawyer warned that member that he better pray about it. That gentleman told our secretary, "Don't be shocked if a sheriff padlocks the doors of Zion Baptist Church."

When that deacon told this in the meeting, I said, "He is on dangerous ground. When you touch God's church, you are touching the apple of God's eye" (Zech. 2:8). When I got home that night, as I was praying, I said, "Lord, you can't let him do that to your church. That is your church." The very next morning, I received a call that this member was in the hospital. I went to visit him and noticed he was really nervous. I didn't mention what I had been told. I didn't want him to have a heart attack. He never got to go home. He died while still in the hospital. He was seventy-three years old. You can't put your hand on God's church and get by.

Another incident was a lady who was sitting on the back pew of the church. She was heard cursing in the church. No one should be cursing, let alone a Christian. Still further, certainly not in the house of God. Soon after, she had a stroke, ended up in the hospital, and then died. She was just forty-six years old; really, she was too young to die. Be careful how you behave in the house of God. 1 Timothy 3:15: "But if I tarry long that thou mayest know how thou oughtest to behave thyself in the house of God," Ecclesiastes 5:1-2 "Keep thy foot when thou goest to the house of God, and be more ready to hear, than to give the sacrifice of fools: for they consider not that they do evil. Be not rash with thy mouth, and let not thine heart be hasty to utter anything before God: for God is in heaven, and thou upon earth: therefore, let thy words be few."

One Sunday morning, I drove the church van, picking up kids, and bringing them to church. Some of the kids were not ready so I told them that I would take the kids I had in the van on to church and to get ready, and I would be back to pick them up. On the way to the church, I passed a woman with a flat tire. There was a man with a jack helping her. I took the kids on to church and went back to get the other kids. I passed the same car with the flat and the same man working on it. After picking up the kids, I went back the same route, and there was the man still working on the woman's flat tire. I couldn't believe that the car was still not jacked up. I stopped and found that the man trying to jack up the car was drunk. He had put the jack under the fender. The fender was bent badly. I said, "You have to put the jack under the frame." I got the car jacked up like it was supposed to be. It is no telling how much that drunkard cost that poor lady to get her fender fixed. The lesson is, don't let drunks work on your car. Better still, don't ever drink. Be a tee-total-er because strong drink is destructive.

I have so many mighty men and women at Zion. Many have passed on to that heavenly country. Rev. Robert Ammons was such a great man. He was happy to be the second man. When I came to Zion, he would take me to visit all the shut-ins. He and Ms. Lillie Bolch did a lot of visiting on their own. His brother, Willard Ammons, was also a faithful soul. He would ring the church bell every Sunday morning. Brother Willard passed away on January 27, 2015, at the age of ninety. Willard's wife Jessie "Bill" passed away on December 26, 2004, at the age of seventy-seven.

Willard & wife Jesse "Bill" Ammons

Rev. Robert Ammons had resigned as assistant pastor before I came to Zion. In the other churches that I pastored, I never had an assistant. Rev. Robert passed away on June 17, 2010, at the age of ninety-one. Ms. Lillie passed away on October 13, 2008, at the age of eighty-seven. Preacher Robert was a great man.

**Left to right: Mary Cash, Hazel Myers, Nancy White, me,
Rev. Robert Ammons, & Lillie Bolch**

In January 2014, the Lord sent me an assistant, Rev. Matthew Mills, and his wife, Jessica, to help us, and they surely were a great blessing. It was so amazing that I held both of them in my arms when they were first born. Both Matt and Jessica's parents attended Zion Hill. Rev. Matt brought some new ideas with him that proved to be a great blessing to us. One was the "One Call" system that every church should have. This system will call every member that signs up for it and gives them an automated message concerning events or prayer request, and other needs. Rev. Matt also began putting my sermons, and his also, on YouTube. Rev. Matt is a great preacher. He was ordained as a pastor in May 2014 at Zion Hill by Rev. Tom Walker. He stayed with us until February 2019, then was called to pastor Cane River Baptist in Burnsville, North Carolina. He is a Billy Graham in the making. While they were with us at Zion Baptist, they had a little boy added to their family, Callen. He brought joy to them and also the church family. Also, Jessica is a great singer.

Rev. Matthew Mills and wife Jessica

104

Brother Kaywood Hale and his wife Edna were pillars in Zion. They were the first ones at our church services. He would encourage people to come to Sunday School and be in the prayer room and also to attend Brotherhood. Kaywood went with me on visitation on Thursday nights. He had several different sayings. One was, "God has been better to me than he was to Hezekiah. God gave Hezekiah fifteen more years, but he gave me thirty years." Kaywood had a heart attack at the age of fifty and lived thirty-seven years more. Another saying Kaywood had was, "I'm going to get that crown for faithfulness; in fact, I've already got it." I'm sure he was right because Kaywood remained faithful until he died. Revelation 2:10 says, "Be thou faithful unto death and I will give thee a crown of life." Kaywood went on visitation with me on Thursday night, then he had a stroke the very next day, and a week later, he passed away on November 10, 2001, at the age of eighty-seven, and his wife Edna passed away on April 21, 2004, at the age of eighty-two. They were faithful Christians.

Kaywood & Edna Hale

Their daughter Thelma and husband Lemuel Whisnant have been pillars at Zion. Brother Lemuel has been in the bus ministry since 1995, bringing kids and grown-ups to the house of God. Also, he plays the electric guitar for the choir and for special singers and has sung a song or two himself. Sister Thelma is an organizer. She leads the women every year in a retreat to Gatlinburg and also in a fundraiser for her Sunday school class. Sister Thelma sang in a group called Zion Trio. My first meal at Zion was cooked by Sister Thelma Whisnant. What a meal she cooked. I asked her, "How did a city girl learn to cook like a country girl?" She said, "I am a country girl." Lemuel was blessed by receiving a heart transplant, for which he gives God the praise.

Thelma & Lemuel Whisnant

Sister Evelyn Williams led the women's retreat to Gatlinburg before Mrs. Thelma started. Mrs. Evelyn and her family have been pillars in Zion. Sister Evelyn has been a member since October 14, 1962. Her husband, Joe "Bullie" Williams, was a deacon at Zion until he passed away on April 22, 1985. Evelyn Williams passed away on January 2, 2021, at the age of eighty-eight.

Evelyn Williams

Sister Evelyn's son, Brother Kenny Williams, has also been a member since October 14, 1962. He is such an encourager, and his wife, Anita, who works the nursery on Sunday mornings. Brother Kenny drove a church bus for years and currently teaches Sunday school. The Williams Family is one of many pillars in Zion.

Kenny Williams & wife Anita

Brother Clyde Wiggins, who is a deacon, and his wife, Helen "Pete" Wiggins, were hard workers and dependable. Sister Pete was such a great worker. She oversaw the kitchen during Jubilee and also the Funeral Food Committee, and if the family was small, she would cook the whole meal herself. She did this until she had a stroke and eventually required skilled nursing in a nursing home. Sister "Pete" passed away on October 1, 2018, at the age of eighty, and has gone on to that heavenly country. Brother Clyde also teaches Sunday school and the Men's Brotherhood and cuts the grass for Zion.

Clyde & Helen (Pete) Wiggins

Brother Larry White, who is also a deacon and Sunday school superintendent, has led the singing at Zion ever since I have been there. His wife Nancy White has played the piano since they joined Zion on March 3, 1982. She plays by ear. A singer can get up with a song they wrote, and she can pick out the tune for it. Brother Bill McCarter said some of the brethren from another church came to Zion during a revival just to hear Nancy play the piano. Their son Jamie White is a deacon at Zion and a Sunday school teacher. The White Family are among the singers at Zion.

Me & Carolyn with the White Family
Men–left to right: Jamie, Caleb, me, Larry
Women – left to right: Carolyn, Michelle, Audrey, Katherine Nancy

Brother Eddie Hallman and his wife Linda have been a great blessing to Zion ever since they joined Zion on March 2, 1986. Eddie drives a van on Sunday mornings, picking up kids and adults, bringing them to God's house. He also teaches a Sunday school class and answers the phone for the TV program on Wednesday nights.

Eddie & Linda Hallman

Linda Hallman and Doris McCarley are such a blessing. They taught Sunday school for the Beginners Class for a long time. They visit our members who are shut-in or sick, in the hospital, and also nursing homes. Linda and Doris have also served on the Funeral Food Committee to organize a meal and comfort families who have lost a loved one. Doris and her husband Tommy joined Zion on March 2, 1986. Brother Tommy passed away on May 1, 2005, at the age of sixty.

Doris & Tommy McCarley

Brother Steve Norket, who has gone on to glory, had such a great way about him. He would call absentees and the sick. He just knew what to say for a word of encouragement. His wife Denise Norket is, at present, the secretary of the church. What a worker and how efficient. She typed and retyped the books that I had printed, *The God of the Bible, Volumes 1 & 2*. Further, she has done a bang-up job on typing this book besides all the other things she does.

Steve & Denise Norket

Zion owes a lot to Joel Reeves for his labors and the materials used in remodeling the kitchen in the Fellowship Building. Joel paid for all the materials used in the remodeling. Still further, he purchased a lot of the utensils used in the cooking.

Thanks to those who helped do the work, George Steel, Eddie Hallman, Steve Norket, Gary Queen, and others. Gary passed away on March 8, 2021, at the age of seventy, and his wife Karen passed away on her birthday, March 10, 2021, at the age of seventy-one.

Karen & Gary Queen

The kitchen has been a great blessing for many of the events that we have had at Zion, especially when we have the "Great Labor Day Jubilee." That kitchen is a "number one" kitchen by the side of any other kitchen.

Brother Joel Reeves and his wife Ruth were tithers and also great "gifters." In fact, we have a lot of great "gifters" at Zion. Ruth never saw a stranger. She had a great personality. Thank God for them. Ruth passed away September 25, 2021 at the age of seventy-one.

Brother Joel passed away on April 6, 2016, at the age of seventy-one and Brother Steve passed away on February 22, 2016, at the age of sixty-six. They have both gone on to be with the "Master Carpenter," Jesus Christ.

George and Marsha Steel have taught the children's church since they came from Zion Hill to Zion Baptist. They attended Zion Hill and taught chil-

Joel & Ruth Reeves

dren's church while I was there. In fact, Marsha was the treasurer at Zion Hill. Also she went with Brother Lemuel to pick up kids every Sunday. People may think that George and Marsha followed us to Zion, but that is not what happened. George was working for Byrd's Electric in Marion, North Carolina, and he got laid off. Mrs. Alma Robinson was a member of Zion, and her son owned an electrical company in Gastonia, so I recommended George to him. Thus, he was hired in Gastonia.

Joel Reeves & Steve Norket in the Zion Fellowship Building

Marsha worked at Bank of America. So she transferred to Bank of America in Charlotte. Thus, they came to Zion to help us out. Thank you, Lord, for sending them!

I don't know if we would have been able to have our first Jubilee had it not been for Brother George. George, being an electrician, knew how to get the electricity run from the electrical pole for the lights, microphones, speakers, TV, and recorders. He also slept in his truck to watch the tent and the piano several times.

George & Marsha Steel

Brother Glenn and Judy Wood are the custodians. They live close by and always open the church doors before each service. They are so faithful. Glenn was also over building maintenance and could repair many things around the church. Brother Glenn passed away on October 15, 2021, at the age of seventy-five.

Glenn & Judy Wood (Custodians)

Still further, there is Brother Danny Cochran and his wife Kathy, who joined Zion on April 28, 2002. Danny and Kathy operate the soundboard and TV camera, a very complicated system that we put in after the ceiling fell in the sanctuary and destroyed our old system. He and Kathy both work like beavers in the Great Labor Day Jubilee.

Still further, he spends a lot of time in editing the TV and radio programs. Kathy is another person who has a super personality. She can do that beautiful writing called calligraphy. Thanks to Danny and Kathy!

Danny & Kathy Cochran

There is Michelle White running the computer for the monitors to keep the congregation informed of announcements, songs, and the Scriptures used during the service.

Left to right: Kathy & Danny Cochran, Michelle White

I couldn't leave out Scott Fish, who has been a faithful friend. When I was at Zion Hill, Scott was a teenager. I had to have surgery. After surgery, he called to check on me. I just got home from the hospital. He said, "How is the preacher?" Carolyn responded, "Oh Scott, he is spoiled." He said, "Don't talk about the preacher." That has been his thinking since he was a teenager.

Scott Fish

Scott Fish came to Zion with his dad, Eddie Fish. He went to the altar that night and got saved. He had been on drugs and alcohol, and God took all that away. He joined Zion and was baptized on May 2, 1998. That is the night that he met Jackie Rhyne. A courtship ensued for about nine months, with Scott driving from Marion, North Carolina to come to Zion and also to see Jackie. Then they married and, eventually, they moved to Clover, South Carolina. They have two children, Breezy and Peyton. Jackie is a nurse, and her Mother Sib Rhyne and sister Tina Eaker sing as a group called "Victory Voices," and Jackie also sings solos.

One Sunday after I came to Zion, I was sick. Scott was driving a church bus at that time. After he let his load off, he called me. He asked if I had Gatorade or Pedialyte or Pepsis to drink. I said, "No, but I will get Carolyn to get some." In just a little while, he knocked on the door with all kinds of those things that I just mentioned. There must have been fifty-dollars' worth of stuff. A friend in need is a friend indeed.

Scott is a number-one mechanic. He has a regular job that he works on. He said the only cars that he will work on are his family's cars, also his cars, and the preacher and Carolyn's cars, and he has done that several different times. Thank God for a friend like that!

I have had three secretaries at Zion. Betty Erwin was my first church secretary from December 1993 to May 1996. Bonnie Hart was my second secretary from April 1996 to December 2004, and Denise Norket has been the secretary since June 2004 when she began filling in for Bonnie Hart, who was out on medical leave. Thank God for good secretaries who keep things running smooth.

Betty Erwin

Brother John Fuller and his wife, Elva, who came back from Robbinsville, North Carolina, have been a great blessing. Brother John does a monthly newsletter called *The Beacon*, which blesses our people, and he also keeps up the Website, zionbc.com. Brother John helped me tremendously with my book, *The God of the Bible*.

Left to Right: Sandra Brittain, me, Carolyn, Elva, & John Fuller

Sister Sandra Brittain kelp things lively at the Chapel Class Fundraiser. She was the life of the party! She liked to surprise people on their birthday and at Christmas time with an unexpected gift. She drove a long way to come to Zion. In fact, we have several members who drive a good, long way to come to Zion. Thank God for them!

Sandra Brittain

Sister Sandra had a big heart. She was so talented. She could sing like a mocking-bird and could shock everybody with an imitation of a crowing rooster. You couldn't tell any difference between her and a rooster. Sandra passed away on August 26, 2021, at the age of seventy-two.

Brother Ronnie Rhom and his wife Judy joined Zion on October 1, 1972. What a worker Ronnie is. He cleaned up all the leftovers of the houses that were burned on our new property, by himself. When our lawn care man was out with his knee, Ronnie cut the grass at the church, parsonage, and the new property for nothing. Anything that I ask Ronnie to do, he will do it. Thank to Brother Ronnie! His wife Judy was a blessing to Zion. She passed away on September 11, 2014, at the age of sixty-nine.

Steven and Tina Eaker's son, Reagan Eaker, helps with the soundboard, TV, camera, and computer system when the others are absent. Reagan's family has been a member of Zion since February 26, 1995.

Steven & Tina Eaker

Reagan Eaker

Tony Jones

There is Tony Jones, our social media editor, who does a great service by keeping up our YouTube and Facebook sites with up-to-date sermons, which is a great outreach. In addition to handling our social media, Tony is also president of the Gaston Radio Club and member of the Amateur Emergency Services and a licensing instructor for the American Radio Relay League.

We have a lot of special singers at Zion. Mary Ball wrote a song about me, titled "Leo Is an Old Time Preacher Man," sung to the tune of Dolly Parton's song, "Daddy Was an Old Time Preacher Man." You can find the words on page 223 of this book. Sandra Brittain, Mike and Teresa Hargrave, Tina Eaker, Jackie Fish, Sib Rhyne, Brenda Mathis, Harvey Spirlin, who passed away on April 22, 2021, at the age of sixty, and Lloyd Dockery and Lisa Mejia are known as Heartfelt. Lloyd always has something funny to say. He is almost a one-man show. He has a tremendous memory. He never looks at a book when singing. He knows all the songs by heart. Further, he memorized the book of Mark chapters 1, 2, and 3 and the book of Revelation chapter 22. Faith Trio (Sandra Brittain, Sib Rhyne, and Carolyn Kuykendall), Victory Voices (Sib Rhyne, Jackie Fish, and Tina Eaker), the White Family (Larry, Nancy, and Jamie White), Zion Trio (Thelma Whisnant, Nancy White, and Jackie Fish). What a blessing to have good singers!

Harvey & Donna Spirlin   **Me & Lloyd Dockery**   **Lisa Mejia & Lloyd Dockery**

There are many more great saints in Zion. They all have a place in the service and ministry of the church.

Mary Ball & husband Albert
(Albert passed away on June 27, 2004, at the age of sixty-nine)

The White Family
Left to Right: Larry, Jamie John, & Nancy

Ministers

I have had several different preachers come through Zion since I have been here. They were a blessing to me, and I hope that I was a blessing to them.

There was Rev. Robert Ammons, who had been the former assistant pastor and filled in while Zion was looking for a pastor. Rev. Ammons was a great man and a great preacher.

Rev. Robert Ammons

Rev. Kenneth Spirlin and his wife Margaret. Rev. Ken had pastored the Brown town Baptist Church in Belmont, North Carolina. Also, he pastored Glory Road Baptist Church before joining Zion Baptist. Rev. Ken passed away on January 6, 1996, at the age of sixty-seven, and his wife Margaret passed away in 1997 at the age of sixty-three.

Rev. Ken & Margaret Spirlin

Rev. David Spirlin and his wife Pat was a blessing to Zion Baptist. David played the piano and sang solos and also had a group called "Homeward Bound Trio," which consisted of David, his wife Pat, and Sandra Brittain. David passed away on Nov 16, 2020, at the age of sixty-seven, and his wife Pat passed away on August 26, 2001, at the age of forty-two.

Left to right: back row – Pat, Rev. David Spirlin, & Tina Spirlin
Front row: Rev. Ken & Margaret Spirlin

Rev. Jake Rhyne and wife Sib. Jake and Sib were longtime members of Zion before Jake announced his call to preach. I ordained Rev. Jake on December 3, 2017, and he became the Pastor of Mill haven Baptist Church in Charlotte, North Carolina, following the death of their former pastor, Rev. Charles Kinley on August 23, 2016, at the age of seventy-four. Rev. Charles Kinley was such a kind and gentle man and also an encourager. He preached for me several times at Zion.

Rev. Charles Kinley   **Rev. Jake Rhyne & Sib**   **Rev. Matthew Mills,**
Jessica, and Callen

Jake and Sib got to be with us on Sunday evenings and Wednesday nights occasionally. Jake's wife Sib and their two daughters, Jackie Fish and Tina Eaker, sing together in a group called "Victory Voices." Sib writes a lot of the songs that they sing.

Rev. Matthew Mills and his wife Jessica who was our youth pastor and assistant pastor from January 5, 2014 until February 17, 2019, when he announced his call to become a full-time pastor. Rev. Matt is now the pastor of Cane River Baptist Church in Burnsville, North Carolina. Matthew's grandparents John and Thelma Trent were great friends to us at Zion Hill.

Rev. Orville Threatt, who drove from Monroe, North Carolina, to be with us. He has preached for me from time to time as well as preaching at other churches.

Me with Rev. Orville Threatt

Rev. John Gordon and wife Sue, who joined Zion on April 20, 2008, and later transferred to Ridgeview Baptist Church in Charlotte on February 16, 2014.

Rev. Zoltan Thornburg and wife Kim, who was our youth pastor from January 24, 2007, until November 14, 2007.

Rev. Mike White and his wife Esther joined Zion on March 6, 2016. Rev. Mike teaches the Willing Workers Sunday school class and preaches for me when I am on vacation, and at other times. He is a fiery preacher, and folks enjoy his preaching. Mike was ordained as a minister on June 6, 2021, at Zion, and Rev. Charles Worley spoke at his ordination. Rev. Mike's wife Esther passed away on January 5, 2021, at the age of sixty-three.

Me, Rev. Charles Worley, Rev. Mike White

Rev. Jeff Cook and his wife Carolyn, who became the pastor of Beech Avenue Baptist Church in Gastonia. They are great singers as a husband and wife and have beautiful harmony.

Rev. Jeff & Carolyn Cook

Rev. Bobby Herndon and wife Ginger, who later became the pastor of Serenity Baptist Church in Gastonia. Every so often, Rev. Bobby calls and gives me a word of encouragement about our TV program, *The Bible Hour*.

Rev. Bobbie & Ginger Herndon

Baptizing

Every pastor has some funny experiences in baptizing new converts. One experience was a lady at Zion. She waded into the baptistery, and just as I was about to baptize her, she said, "Wait a minute," and she turned and pulled her billfold out of her bosom. She said, "I don't want my money to get wet." Everyone in the congregation laughed. It certainly was funny.

Another lady came into the baptistery. She was short, and the water almost came up to her chin. She grabbed hold of the baptistery glass and started walking across the baptistery, talking. I don't know if she was just talking or testifying, but she kept heading back the way she came in. I said, "Wait a minute, I haven't baptized you yet."

Another time was when a man who didn't have legs wanted to be baptized. I had never baptized anyone with that handicap. I got a wooden stool to set him on and held my foot on it. One of the deacons, Brother Ronald Davidson, carried him into the baptismal pool and sat him on the stool. When I baptized him, I took my foot off the stool, and his weight came off the stool, and it popped up to the surface. Brother Ronald and I grabbed him to keep him from going under.

When I was at Good News, we did not have a baptistery, so we baptized in Enka Lake, now called Biltmore Lake, just outside of Asheville, North Carolina. Mrs. Thelma Baldwin made things right and joined the church. She then wanted to be baptized. She had emphysema really bad. She said the doctor told her not to get a cold. This was the first baptizing of the year, and the weather wasn't very warm. She didn't know whether to be baptized at this time or not. I told her it was up to her, to pray about it, and do what the Lord told her to do. She decided that she would be baptized. The water was cold when I walked in, and when I put her under and brought her up, it seemed like it took a minute for her to catch her breath. In the night service, she told me, "I wished that I had been baptized a long time ago. I feel so good." I have never heard of anyone getting sick after they were baptized, even though the water may be cold as ice.

Another occasion was when I was at Zion Hill. We didn't have a baptismal pool until we built the new church. Before that, we baptized in Buck Creek out of Marion, North Carolina, which came right out of the mountain and usually was very cold. At this particular baptizing, when I baptized my last candidate, I said something that I never say. I said, "Is there anyone here that is not satisfied with their baptism?" Mr. Roy Buchanan, who was wearing a suit, came kicking off his shoes and pulling off his coat and said, "I never have been satisfied with my baptism. I didn't have confidence in the preacher that baptized me, and I want you to baptize me." Thus, after I baptized him, he was satisfied. Mr. Buchanan died in 1995 at the age of eighty-three.

I was raised in the mountains, and a lot of those old-fashioned churches did not believe in baptismal pools. They believed you ought to be baptized in running water. One of our members built a new swimming pool and invited us to use his pool for our baptizing. That was also at Zion Hill, before we built the new church. What I discovered was that water is water, whether it is in a river or a lake or a pool; water is water the world around. It was a super baptizing.

Of course, baptizing signifies the death, burial, and resurrection of Christ. It is a testimony to the world that you believe Jesus died and was buried and rose on the third day from the dead. It is also saying to the world that you have died out to sin and that you have buried the old life and have arisen to walk a new life in Christ Jesus. Baptizing does not wash away your sins. Revelation 1:5 says, "Unto him that loved us and washed us from our sins in his own blood." Also, First John 1:7 says that " the blood of Jesus Christ his son cleanseth us from all sin."

Brother Horace Beavers & Ethel joined Zion on June 26, 2005, in the morning service, and Mr. Beavers was baptized in the evening service. Mr. Beavers said, "I thought a man shouldn't cry until I saw the preacher cry." Then he said, "If it's alright for the preacher to cry, then it's alright for me to cry." Kenny Williams was an active deacon at that time and helped in the baptizing. When I baptized Mr. Beavers, he came up shouting and almost lost his teeth. I told him his son Todd (who passed away on December 30, 2004, at the age of thirty-six) that he was shouting over in heaven. Mr. Beavers passed away on March 31, 2008, at the age of seventy.

Then there was Truman Bitzel. Truman's wife, Carol, joined Zion Baptist on July 27, 1997. Truman came with Carol but didn't join at that time. Years later, Truman became ill and was in and out of the hospital. In 2011, I went to visit him while he was in the hospital. I gave him the plan of salvation and prayed with him. When I finished praying, Truman began to pray. Truman gave his heart to Christ that day in the hospital. Every time that I prayed with Truman and finished, then he would pray. He is the only person that I ever remember doing that. Truman joined Zion Baptist on September 18, 2011. He was to be baptized the next Sunday after he joined, but he had to go back to the hospital. He was never able to come back to church. Truman passed away on June 21, 2012, at the age of seventy.

Carol & Truman Bitzel

Prayer Warriors

The Lord is so good to me, and I am sure that he is to every God-called preacher. In that, He lays a burden on the hearts of His people to pray for preachers. I can't tell you of all the people that have said, "I pray for you every day."

Mr. Talmadge Medford was Papaw Medford's brother. He told me, "I pray for you every day." I hardly knew him, but the Lord put that on his heart. Talmadge passed away on July 8, 1981, at the age of eighty-three.

Shirley Pitman told us that she prays for us every day. All that I can do is bow my head and say, "Lord, I surely need their prayers. Thank you, Lord, for taking care of your servant!"

Brother Bob Pitman, whom I have mentioned in these papers, had a preacher friend who lives in Georgia, Rev. Darrell Weaver. He had told Rev. Weaver about me being his friend. From that time, Rev. Weaver prays for me every day. With all his activities, he still took time to call my name to the Lord in prayer. Is that a blessing or what? Yes, what a blessing! He pastored a church in Florida for several years. He now lives in Baxley, Georgia, and pastors Faith Baptist Church. He is a great preacher, singer, and a guitarist.

Rev. Darrell Weaver & wife Wanda

I have had others who have said, "I pray for you every day." It is the Lord who puts that burden in their hearts.

Amazing People

In my Christian life, I have met some wonderful Christian men. I say, really, they are spiritual giants. One was called Grandpa Presnell. He was in his seventies or eighties. He would smack his hands together and say, "They call me a holy roller, but I am rolling toward the city." That city was heaven.

Another was called Grandpa Lunsford. He was in his eighties. They would call on him to pray in the service. He would get on his knees and pray and then come up preaching and praising the Lord.

Both of these men who were in their seventies and eighties were still bringing forth fruit in their old age (Ps. 92:14).

Then there was Theodore Odear. He was an older gentleman who was somewhat crippled in his feet. But he ran a farm for a doctor whose practice was in Canton. He was uneducated and could not read, but he certainly had the power of God on his life. He would stand and give a testimony in the service and close his testimony with, "Pray for me that I will become more peculiar."

Rev. Doug Hall was a boy who I went to school with. He was one grade behind me. He went to Mission Hospital to visit some of his members. When he parked his car, he saw a policewoman writing tickets on expired meters. So, Doug went ahead of her, putting money in the expired meters. He got such a blessing he started shouting there on the street. Someone took a picture of him praising the Lord and put it in the Asheville Times Newspaper.

I remember two great instances of hospitality that happened to me. When I was working with Nelson Hinson, cutting hay, I was raking hay at that time. It was hot, and the hay was dusty. Here came Preacher Peak out in the field with a big glass of ice water to give me. Man, what a blessing. I never ever heard him preach, but I can say that he was given to hospitality.

On another occasion, when I worked for Southern Bell, I was putting a phone in a trailer. It was hot, and I was sweating profusely. The trailer door came open, and the lady who lived there came out with a big glass of iced tea. Up until that time, I did not like iced tea, but I did not tell her that I didn't drink iced tea. I thanked her for it and drank that delicious iced tea. From that day until today, I love iced tea because a lady was given to hospitality.

Mrs. Maggie Roland was married to Rev. John Roland. She was one of Rev. Roland's converts, and he also baptized her. When she married Rev. Roland, she was younger than his children from a previous marriage, but she loved him very much. When he was sick in the hospital, she sat beside his bed, day and night. He died very close to the time I went to Good News. Further, she was one of those shouting saints who was not ashamed to praise the Lord, which is hard to find in our generation. What is so special about Mrs. Roland was that she was very poor. She lived in just a poor-looking house and lived on a fixed income. Every Sunday as she went out the door of the church after the service was over, she would put a dollar in my hand for the *Bible Hour* radio broadcast. I said, "Mrs. Roland, you need this money more than I do." Her daughter, Myrtle Catchot, was behind her and said, "Don't cheat her out of a blessing." She gave me a dollar every Sunday. There were people in the church who had a lot more money than her, but did not give. Another special thing is the way she died. One evening, she cooked her supper and then cut off the stove, sat down on the couch to watch the news, and the Lord called her home to heaven. She didn't die in the hospital or in a nursing home. She died in peace at home. Rev. Roland passed away on November 29, 1969, at the age of ninety-five. Maggie passed away on March 31, 1980, at the age of seventy-nine. Their daughter Myrtle passed away on September 18, 1991, at the age of sixty-nine.

Revivals

Years ago, when I was attending Gardner Webb College, after class, I went on to WAGI Radio in Gaffney, South Carolina to take radio tapes. I was praying about the Lord using me. The Lord said that he would use me in revivals. After that, I preached a lot of revivals. God always keeps his word.

One great revival experience was when I went with the Rock of Ages Prison Ministry to the Kentucky State Penitentiary, which is Kentucky's oldest and only maximum-security facility that houses Kentucky's death row inmates. The facility houses 856 inmates. There were several preachers who participated in this revival. We went from cell to cell, witnessing. One thing that amazed me was many inmates said they were Muslims. I thought that was a religion mostly of the Middle East. Yet, that belief had infiltrated into that prison. I believe that the Muslim religion will be the religion of the antichrist.

Kentucky State Penitentiary

When it was my turn to preach, I preached a sermon entitled "Can God Change You," out of the book of Jeremiah 13:23. A year or two later, Dr. Ed Ballew was with me in a revival and told me that Dr. Ron Gearis (who was a missionary evangelist with the Rock of Ages Prison Ministry and later became their president in 1987), had been preaching that message in a lot of prisons and winning a lot of souls with it. At first, I became angry that he was preaching my sermon. But then the Lord said, "That is dividends." Thank to Dr. Gearis, for preaching that sermon and winning a lot of souls! Dr. Gearis passed away on September 12, 2006, at the age of sixty-seven.

Dr. Ron Gearis

At Zion Hill, a lady named Marie Mills would write down my sermon outlines and give them to a Freewill Baptist pastor who worked with her. One day, I saw the pastor at the grocery store. He told me about Marie bringing him outlines of my sermons. He said, "I hope you don't mind me preaching them." I told him to help himself, preach them, and win a lot of souls. This will be dividends at the "Judgment Seat"!

I was preaching a revival for Rev. Bobby "Hoot" Gibson at Cedar Mountain Baptist Church in Fairview, North Carolina just outside of Asheville. As I was going to the service one evening, I noticed a billboard announcing the revival with my name all the way across it. What a way to advertise a revival with a billboard! Rev. Gibson passed away on June 13, 2019, at the age of eighty-eight years old.

Cedar Mountain Baptist Church billboard announcing me to preach a revival

On another occasion, my brother-in-law, James Wilson, called me and asked me to come preach a revival at his church. I said, "When do you want me to come?" He said, "Either the first or second week of the month." He said, "I will talk to the men and get back with you." Later, he called back and said, "The second." On Monday night, April 2, 1990, I was lying in bed, and my sister, Mary Lou, called and said, "Where are you?" I said, "In bed." She said, "You were supposed to preach here tonight." It just so happened that that Monday night, when revival was to start, was the second day of the month. I thought he meant the second week. The lesson here is to be sure that you are clear on the date and on the time for any appointment.

Rev. Bobby "Hoot" Gibson

I preached a "Watch Night" service for Rev. Wayne Blanton at Bright Light Baptist Church in Bessemer City, North Carolina. Later, I went back and preached a revival for him. An unusual thing happened. One night, in the meeting, I preached on hell. A lady started shouting at the back of the church and shouted all the way to the front of the church and all the way back to her seat. I had never seen that before, nor have I seen it since. The only thing that I surmise is that she was glad she was not going to hell. Later, I had Rev. Blanton preach a revival for me at Zion Hill. He was the most "shouting preacher" that I had ever seen. Thank God for spiritual men like that.

I had heard many things about Evangelist Ed Kuykendall before I ever met him. We probably are kin, but it would be a distant cousin. I heard a few things about him; one was he was preaching a revival, and it was summertime. All the windows of the church were opened. There was no air conditioners back in those days. The singing was completed, so the pastor got up and said, "It is time for preaching to begin, but the preacher is not here." About that time, Ed Kuykendall jumped in the church through one of the open windows. At another revival, he came in the church dragging a log chain. Still further, another time when he got up to preach, he said, "I was walking through the parking lot, and I saw Buicks, Pontiacs, Chevrolets, and one old dilapidated Ford." Then he asked, "Who owned that dilapidated Ford?" Someone said, "It belongs to the pastor." Evangelist Ed said, "That's just what I thought. You don't want a revival." He closed his Bible and walked out. In other words, the way you treat God's man is the way you treat God (Acts 9:4–5; Matt. 26:37–40, 45).

While at Rock of Ages Conference in Cleveland, Tennessee, I went to visit Evangelist Ed Kuykendall in Hixson, Tennessee. We sat on his porch, and he preached to me for an hour and a half. He told me that at one time, he was booked in revivals for twelve years, which is unheard of, but that is what he told me. He also told me that he had twenty-five sermons on hell. I asked him if he had any sons, and he said, "No." Then I asked him if I could have them when he died. But sadly, I never talked to him again, nor did I know when he died. Preacher Ed had retired at that time. We saw the birds hopping around in the yard while we sat on the porch. He said, "I am not going to worry about how to make it; when I see the birds worrying, then I will begin worrying."

Rev. Luther Spivey and I have had a lot of great times together. I preached revivals in four different Churches that Rev. Spivey had pastored. One at Chestnut Ridge in

Fairview, NC, Cedar Hill in Leicester, NC, Bee Log Baptist in Burnsville, NC and Sullins Branch in Spruce Pine, NC. Rev. Spivey is a great preacher. He preaches with power and with tears. Every Church he pastored grew under his ministry. Rev. Spivey left pastoring and went to Mexico as a Missionary in 1999, which Zion had a part in supporting him. He organized 172 Churches in Mexico. He has of late been installed as the General Manager of the KJV Radio Ministry on 1380 AM in Asheville, NC. Rev. Spivey is fighting cancer. They gave him three to six months to live. By God's grace it has been 4 years and he is still going strong. The Doctor said to him, "You are doing great"! He is still working with Pastor's in Mexico.

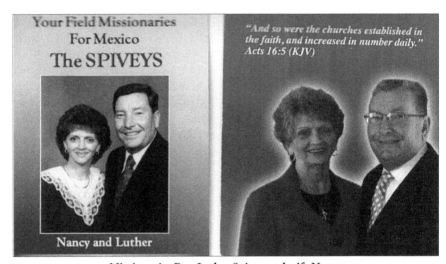

Missionaries Rev. Luther Spivey and wife Nancy

A dear preacher friend of mine was Rev. Granville L. Kilby. He came to Good News Baptist to hear me preach. I preached on "A Cake Not Turned" out of the book of Hosea chapter 7:8. It was not long after that Rev. Kilby asked me to preach a revival for him at Roland's Chapel Baptist Church in Nebo, North Carolina. In fact, I preached four revivals for him, two of which were at Crabtree Baptist in Burnsville, North Carolina. I preached a total of four revivals at Crabtree Baptist in Burnsville, North Carolina. I preached two revivals for Rev. Kilby and two revivals for Rev. Claude Surrett. Also, I preached a revival for Rev. Kilby at Forge Valley Baptist Church in Mills River. I enjoyed my fellowship and labors with Rev. Kilby. Rev. Kilby passed away on October 26, 1999, at the age of eighty-three.

He had three sons, Gary Kilby, Roy, who has pastored Bethel Baptist for over forty years, and his son Randy, who was only a teenager when I preached the revival at Roland's Chapel. Later, Randy became the sixth president of Fruitland Baptist Bible College. Randy's last sermon was preached at the West Lenoir Baptist Bible Conference. Pastor James Lockey was the pastor. Randy preached and then went to his room to change shirts. He didn't come back, so someone went to check on him, and he had passed away. From the pulpit to heaven; I don't think you can beat that. Randy passed away on February 11, 1997, at the age of forty-two.

Carolyn and I went to the same church, as did Benny Metcalf and his wife Doris. That church was Mt. Pisgah Baptist Church. Benny announced his call to preach. Pastor Bill Belcher would let him preach now and then. Benny would preach only about five minutes every time he preached. People began to wonder if he had been called to preach. One night in the Men's Prayer Room, before the service, the Spirit fell on Benny. He got up preaching and went out to the pulpit preaching and preached for about thirty minutes before he stopped. From that time on, he could preach. Benny pastored several different churches before he retired. Rev. Benny was also a great singer. One of the songs that he sang, which I thoroughly enjoyed, was "More About Jesus I Would Know."

Rev. Daniel Sexton was Nancy White's dad. She is our pianist and her husband Larry is the song leader. Rev. Sexton loved to sing and did a great job. Rev. Sexton and his family sang at many churches. He was a joy to be around. I enjoyed the jokes and stories he told. Rev. Sexton slipped away on August 2, 2010, at the age of eighty-one. Nancy's mom, Mildred Sexton, passed away on November 7, 2006, at the age of seventy-six.

Left to right: Rev. Dan Sexton, Rev. Bennie Metcalf, & wife Doris

I have learned a few things by experience as a pastor over the years. One is when the Spirit is moving in the service, it is best not to try to preach. In other words, people are being blessed and testifying, and there is a sweet spirit. Let the Lord have his way. There have been a few times that I tried to preach in a service like that, and it turned out to be a dead service. As I tell them, "When the Big Preacher comes, the little preacher (pastor) sits down." When the Spirit is moving, just let him have his way.

Further, I have learned things from every pastor that I have sat under. As the old saying goes, "Any old mule knows to eat the hay (gets the good points) and not the briars (the bad points)."

Rev. Dave Walton – Rev. Don Stanley
They took a night about preaching in revival at Zion Hill.

Don Stanley had been in prison and was released. After that, Don and Dave established a halfway house in Spartanburg, South Carolina, to help those released from prison. They bought an old school house that needed a lot of renovation work Several of the men from Zion Hill and myself went down to help them one Saturday. Dave and Don had a big job ahead of them before they would be ready for their first inmate.

Vacation Bible Schools

Not long after I came to Zion in Gastonia, we were running eight buses on Sunday. So, at VBS time, each bus captain visited kids on his own route. Plus, we had other members knocking on doors, inviting kids to come for VBS. In June 1994, we had our first Vacation Bible School at Zion with me as pastor. We had 233 kids and 22 workers.

VBS Bus Ministry

At Vacation Bible School in 1995, we had 527 kids and 89 workers. We didn't have enough rooms to accommodate that many kids, and the rooms we had were not big enough to seat all that we had. All of our classes were filled to capacity and over. It overworked all of the volunteers, and we had head lice that kids had caught at school. After commencement night, the workers said, to me, "We are not going to help you anymore."

Me & Thelma Whisnant as the devil for VBS
Sword = Word of God

So, the next year, 1996, we had a more manageable group, 266 kids and 42 workers. However, our workers were getting fewer and fewer. In 1997, we were back up to 431 kids and just 46 workers. We had the pink eye at this VBS. In 1998, we had 363 kids and 47 workers.

So, in 1999, we went to a one-day, Saturday, VBS. We had 178 kids and 54 workers that year. A few years after that, we went to a three-day VBS. Friday night, all day Saturday, and commencement on Sunday night. This was much better for the workers. We continued doing a three-day VBS until 2013. That year, we did not have enough volunteers, so we took a rest.

In 2014, we had "Tricky Ricky" Henson, a ventriloquist, to do a "Family & Kid Crusade" for VBS. It started on Sunday night and ended Wednesday night with the commencement service. Brother Ricky could hold their attention with his Christian stories and illusions. It was such a relief to all the workers. Brother Ricky did our VBS for five years. Then, in 2019, we went back to the three-day VBS. Unfortunately, we were unable to have VBS in 2020 due to the coronavirus pandemic known as COVID-19.

Evangelist Ricky Henson & me

Jubilees

Rev. Ralph Sexton, Sr. in Asheville, North Carolina, had a one-night Jubilee on Labor Day at Trinity Baptist Church. He changed the Jubilee to a one-week Bible conference, called the "Land of the Sky Jubilee." That is when I began the "Great Labor Day Jubilee" in 1985. I had nine Jubilees before I left Zion Hill, and I continued that tradition when I moved to Zion Baptist Church in Gastonia, North Carolina.

As of this writing, we have had twenty-six Jubilees in Gastonia, North Carolina. The first Jubilee at Zion Baptist was on September 4, 1994. The Great Labor Day Jubilee is always the Sunday night before Labor Day, which is on Monday. A fifty-foot by one-hundred-foot tent is set up in the parking lot with 500 chairs, and the church and Fellowship Hall are open with TV monitors inside for any overflow seating. The Jubilee starts at 7:00 pm, (officially) and goes to about 11:00 pm (or when all the singers have sung and all the preachers have preached). We usually have three groups of singers and three preachers. It is the greatest service we have the whole year. It is the cherry on top of the icing. The Jubilee is always an exciting time for Zion and for people outside of Zion. It takes a lot of work before the Sunday service and also the day after, to take everything down. But it is worth all the effort.

Jubilee tent set up in Zion parking lot

Under Jubilee tent – seats 500

There have been some great preachers speak at the Jubilee; Dr. Louis Grant—Asheville, North Carolina, Rev. Charles Worley—Maiden, North Carolina, Dr. Ralph Sexton Jr.—Asheville, North Carolina, Dr. Phil Kidd-Kingsport—Tennessee, Rev. Barry Spears—Lugoff, South Carolina, Rev. Rev. Toby Brogden—Ooletewah, Tennessee, Rev. James Lockey—Lenoir, North Carolina, Rev. Larry Sprouse—Alexander, North Carolina, Rev. Bob Mcurry—Buladean, North Carolina, Rev. Daniel Buchanan—Valdese, North Carolina (see picture below), Rev. Leonard Fletcher—Mountain City, Tennessee, and Rev. Wade Huntley—Forest City, North Carolina; great men of God and great preachers.

Rev. Daniel Buchanan
A giant in size and in spirit

Rev. Leonard Fletcher
Pastor of Dyson Grove Baptist Church

Rev. Barry Spears
Pastor of Sonrise Baptist Church

I have known Dr. Louis Grant for many years. In fact, I knew his dad, Rev. Wesley Grant. I was a teenager when I heard Rev. Wesley Grant preach at Welcome Hill Baptist Church in Canton, North Carolina. I still remember what he preached, which was "The Handwriting on the Wall" out of the book of Daniel. Rev. Wesley was a well-known Black preacher in Western North Carolina. He preached in a lot of White churches. I remember him raising money for missionaries in Jamaica for them to buy mules to carry their goods up in the mountains. Still further, I had Rev. Wesley Grant come and preach on Sunday evening at the McDowell Camp Meeting (I was a moderator at that time). It was the biggest crowd that I had ever seen at a Sunday evening service. The tabernacle was full.

Rev. Wesley Grant's son, Louis Grant, has been preaching for me on Sunday morning and also Sunday evening in the Jubilee for at least twenty-six Jubilees. Also, he always sings a song or two. Further, he always stays to the end of the service and helps stack the chairs back on the pallets for the tent company to pick up on Monday following the Jubilee. I asked the young people, "Who do you like the best of all the preachers that I have for Jubilee?" Rev. Louis Grant is their favorite.

Me with Rev. Louis Grant & wife Sandra

I was preaching at the one-night revival at Rev. Ken Burleson's church, Faith Baptist in Marion, North Carolina. I was preaching that in heaven, everything is going to be white, white hair, white garments, and white horses. Rev. Louis Grant, a Black preacher, who was always one of the speakers at this revival, said, "O' Lordy!" I guess he thought what I was saying was everybody in heaven will be White. No, that is not the case. God is a God of variety. Revelation 7:9 says, "After this I beheld, and lo, a great multitude, which no man could number, of all 1. nations 2. and kindreds 3. and people 4. and tongues, stood before the throne, and before the Lamb, clothed with white robes, and palms in their hands." All races are God's creation, and all will be represented there.

Rev. Louis Grant preaching at Jubilee

Let me say a few words about Dr. Phil Kidd, pastor of Emmaus Baptist Church in Kingsport, Tennessee. Rev. Frank Dalton played a lot of Dr. Kidd's sermons on his radio program that he had on WLTC Radio. So, I had heard a lot of Dr. Kidd's preaching. It was not until I heard his testimony that I had him come and preach in the Jubilee. If you have never heard his testimony, you can find it at www.drphilkidd.com and on MP3 audio sermons by Evangelist Phil Kidd at https://godlovespeople.com. What a tremendous testimony. It will have you crying, and it will have you laughing. Dr. Kidd is one of the most powerful preachers that you will ever hear. He is gun-barrel straight. Also, he is as mannerly and respectful as any preacher that I have ever met.

Dr. Phil Kidd

The Joyaires from Harriman, Tennessee, have been with us every year since 1994, singing in the Jubilees. They are not only great singers, but also very spiritual singers with a great testimony.

We've also had the Singing Cooks—Kingsport, Tennessee, Phillips Family—Gaffney, South Carolina, Hayes Family—Boone, North Carolina, Benton Family—Kingsport, Tennessee, Jimmy Justice Family—Hendersonville, North Carolina, Perry Sisters—Huntington, West Virginia, Fraley Family—Bessemer City, North Carolina, the Rowlands—Knoxville, Tennessee, Cross Reference—Kings Mountain, North Carolina, Galloway Family—Brevard, North Carolina, Gospelaires—Mooresville,

North Carolina, Daren and Brooke Aldridge—Cherryville, North Carolina, Fletcher Family—Mountain City, Tennessee. The Redeemed—Rogersville, Tennessee. All of these groups are excellent gospel singers.

The singing Cooks were always a great blessing. I was sad by the news that Hubert Cooke of the Singing Cooks passed away. He died March 12, 2018, at the age of eighty-three.

Singing Groups I've Had at Jubilee

The Singing Cooks
& Cooke Brothers,
Kingsport, Tennessee

The Phillips Family
Gaffney, South Carolina

The Hayes Family Singers
Boone, North Carolina

Benton Family Singers
Kingsport, Tennessee

The Jimmy Justice Family
Hendersonville,
North Carolina

The Perry Sisters
Ceredo, West Virginia

Cross Reference
Kings Mountain, North Carolina

The Gospelaires
Mooresville, North Carolina

Daren & Brooke Aldridge
Cherryville, North Carolina

The Fletcher Family
Mountain City, Tennessee

The Bledsoes

Zion Singers at Jubilee

**Faith Trio: Carolyn Kuykendall—
Sandra Brittain—Sib Rhyne**

**Victory Voices—Jackie Fish—
Tina Eaker—Sib Rhyne**

**Zion Trio—Nancy White—Jackie Fish—
Thelma Whisnant**

Singers I've had sing through the years

The Band Jubilee
Candace, Georgia, Johanna, & Judah Buggay

Georgia, me, Johanna Buggay

The Inspirations

Gospelaires
Me, Rick & Susan Campbell, Carolyn, Chris Sloan

Joe Isaac Family Singers

The Shireys
Darlene, Wayne, & daughter Rachel Flowers

Victoria Shirey Bowlin

Narrow way Quartet

Me & Mike Upright

Brent Rochester Family Singers

Mercy's Well

The Payne Family
Candler, North Carolina

The Fitch Family
Milan, Tennessee

Driven Quartet

The Far City Boys

Mountain Joy

The Potters Clay

Keith Plott

The Primitives

We have had the Primitives from Candler, North Carolina, sing for us here at Zion in Gastonia, numerous times. When we had dedication day for the new church at Zion Hill in Marion, North Carolina, in 1984, the Primitives were the featured guests. It was a great day. My knowing them goes way back to the Wilson Family Singers. There was Rev. Radford Wilson, the dad, Furman Wilson, Norman Wilson, and Ronald Crane. One night the Wilson boys and the Riddle boys went camping, and Reagan took his guitar. Around the camp fire, they learned two songs. The next Sunday, they sang in church. A visitor was there and invited them to his church for a singing, and then from there, soon, they were getting invitations to sing at other churches. There was Reagan Riddle, Larry Riddle, Mike Riddle, Norman Wilson, and Furman Wilson. Later, Rev. Radford Wilson started a new church, called Bethsaida. In the meantime, Furman answered the call to preach, so he left the Primitives and became the pastor of Bethesda Missionary Baptist Church. Rev. Furman Wilson passed away on July 2, 2013, at the age of seventy-one.

The Primitives' music and their harmony was loved everywhere they went, not only their music and their harmony, but also their love and dedication to the Lord and their church, Maple Ridge Baptist Church. In 1981, they began what is called the "Hominy Valley Gospel Singing." It is an outside singing that they have twice a year. Their singing grounds is a beautiful place with Hominy Creek running right through it. You can sit on the porch of my house and hear them singing, for it is just across the field from my house. The Riddle family and the Wilson family were very religious families.

Brother Norman Wilson, who played the mandolin and was the original and only tenor for the Primitive Quartet, was hunting bear with friends in the North Carolina mountains of Graham County when he had a heart attack in the woods. His last words were, "I'm doing exactly what I wanted to do," then he laid down on the ground and was gone. Norman passed away on October 15, 2014, at the age of seventy. You can watch the homegoing service on livestream.com from Trinity Baptist Church in Asheville, North Carolina.

Norman Wilson—tenor for Primitive Quartet

Bible Schools, Institutes, & Colleges

During my time at Good News Baptist Church, I had gone to the Mt. Pisgah Baptist Bible Institute. Rev. Ray Long was the founder and a great teacher. He was also a powerful preacher. I enjoyed hearing him preach many times. I was privileged to ride with him to a revival that he preached in South Carolina. On that ride, he told me something that I never have forgotten. He said, "Leo, you will never enjoy preaching like we did years ago. We could preach against anything and as long as we wanted too and as loud as we wanted too, and they would shout you down, but not today."

Rev. Ray Long

Then, I went to Fruitland Bible Institute in Hendersonville, North Carolina for two years. I later went to Tabernacle Baptist College in Greenville, South Carolina, where I graduated. When I went to Tabernacle in Greenville, I was privileged to sit under Dr. Harold Sightler. Dr. Sightler was a great preacher. He founded Tabernacle Baptist Church, Tabernacle Christian School, Tabernacle Baptist College, Tabernacle Children's Home, Tabernacle Baptist Missions International, a widow's home, and WTBI "The Bright Spot Hour" a daily radio broadcast. Dr. Sightler was on the radio for fifty-five years. He preached revivals every week and taught at the Bible institute. Dr. Sightler passed away on September 27, 1995, at the age of eighty-one. I also sat under Dr. Russell Rice, who passed away on August 3, 2008, at the age of seventy-one, and Dr. E. F. Rabine. Dr. Rabine was a converted Lutheran, and when you came out of his class, you felt like you had been in revival. Dr. John Waters and Dr. Melvin Aiken also were my teachers.

Dr. Harold B. Sightler

When I was going to Tabernacle Baptist Institute, it was an hour-and-a-half drive to school. In my Bible class, studying the book of Hebrews, the teacher would give a test by leaving different words out of the chapter, which the test was on. The only way to make a 100 on a test was to memorize that chapter. By the grace of God, I memorized eleven chapters in the book of Hebrews. I have since lost most of those chapters except Hebrews eleven. I challenge young people to memorize the Scripture while you are young. Keep going over those Scriptures that you memorize. Psalm 119:11 says, "Thy word have I hid in mine heart, that I might not sin against thee." Also, Psalm 1:1 says, "Blessed is the man that (v2) . . . His delight is in the law of the Lord and His law doth he meditate day and night." Also, read Psalm 19:7-11 "The law of the Lord is perfect, converting the soul: the testimony of the Lord is sure, making wise the simple. The statues of the Lord are right, rejoicing the heart: the commandment of the Lord is pure, enlightening the eyes. The fear of the Lord is clean, enduring forever: the judgements of the Lord are true and righteous altogether. More to be desired are they than gold, yea, than much fine gold: sweeter also than honey and the honeycomb. More over by them is the servant warned: and in keeping of them there is great reward."

After, I became the pastor of Zion Hill Baptist Church in Marion, North Carolina. I attended and graduated from Gardner Webb College. I attended there part-time, so it took me six years to finish.

During that time, I was preaching four times a week. Sunday morning, Sunday night, Wednesday night, and a weekly radio program on Sundays. That wasn't all. I was preaching revivals, doing two visitations a week, Thursday Night and Saturday, and hospital visitations. As I look back on it now, I ask myself the question, "How did I do all that?" The only answer is that the Lord gave me the strength to do it. Sometimes I would get overwhelmed with all that I was doing. I would go to my advisor, Dr. Vann Murrell, and I would say, "Dr. Murrell, I'm going to have to drop out for a while." Dr.

Vann Murrell would say, "Keep your hand in the pie, keep your hand in the pie; if you drop out, you will never come back." I took his advice and finished college. I never dropped out. Rev. Vann Murrell passed away on October 31, 2019, at the age of ninety.

Dr. Vann Murrell

While in college, I would sometimes sit up to way in the morning hours, writing and typing term papers. Yes, in those early years, I did my own typing with a typewriter, not a computer. In the last year of college, I wised up and paid someone a dollar a page to type term papers for me. What a relief!

**Getting ready for graduation from Gardner Webb College
At corner of Old Zion Hill Church**

Also in Gardner Webb, I met some men who would turn out to be great preachers. One was Dr. Johnny Hunt, who became the pastor of First Baptist Church Woodstock, in Woodstock, Georgia, and also became the president of the Southern Baptist Convention.

Dr. Johnny Hunt
President of the Southern Baptist Convention

Another was Evangelist Dr. Ron Lynch, who pastored twenty-five years and then went into full-time evangelism out of his desire for revival. He established "LIFE out of DEATH" Ministries in Carolina Shores, North Carolina. I am sure there were others who I have lost touch with that God is using.

Dr. Ron Lynch
"LIFE out of DEATH Ministries"

Meetings & Conferences

The Lord has blessed me to be involved with camp meetings. I was the moderator of the Western North Carolina Camp Meeting in Candler, North Carolina, until I moved to Marion, North Carolina. I had Dr. Percy Ray from Myrtle, Mississippi, and Dr. Kenneth Ridings, who pastored Ebenezer in Hendersonville, North Carolina

at that time. Dr. Ridings was a professor at Fruitland Baptist Bible College. Later, he became the seventh president of Fruitland Baptist Bible College. At that camp meeting, Dr. Ridings preached the whole week on the 23rd Psalm. What preaching. Dr. Ridings passed away on March 5, 2015, at the age of seventy-eight.

Then, one time, I went to Granite Falls Camp Meeting and heard Rev. Bob Marshall preach on the 23rd Psalm. He preached an hour and a half. When he finished, he was dripping wet with sweat. When he walked, you could hear the swishing of water in his shoes. What powerful preaching! Rev. Marshall was the founding pastor of Grace Tabernacle Reformed Baptist Church in Brevard, North Carolina. Rev. Marshall passed away on January 27,

Dr. Kenneth W. Ridings

2014, at the age of seventy-nine.

Brother Wade Huntley, pastor of Holly Springs Baptist Church in Rutherford, North Carolina, also was on the list. Brother Wade built three church buildings while at Holly Springs Baptist. Wade came from a home of four preachers. He built a nursing home and started WWOL Radio Station in Forest City.

All these men were great preachers. What a privilege to rub shoulders with such great men and sit under their preaching. Rev. Huntley passed away on July 23, 2015, at the age of eighty-eight.

Then I was the moderator of the Nebo Camp Meeting for two years. During that time, we poured the floor with concrete. It had been sawdust on the floor. It was not level, and with some of the chairs, you felt like you had to hold on. When we poured the floor, some said, "We can never have a spiritual service again." I said, "There are streets of gold in heaven;

Rev. Wade Huntley

you mean to tell me you can't shout and praise the Lord on concrete? How then will you be able to shout on streets of gold?" All people need to do is read and believe the Bible.

Bus Conferences

I have had the privilege of attending the Bus conferences at Gospel Light Baptist Church in Walkertown, North Carolina, many times, which was always challenging. Also, I've attended countless "Sword of the Lord" conferences, which were always a blessing.

Pastor's School

Further still, I have attended the Pastor's School at the First Baptist Church of Hammond, Indiana several times. I first heard of Dr. Jack Hyles through the Sword of the Lord newspaper. I went to Tabernacle Baptist in Greenville, South Carolina, to hear him for the first time. Dr. Hyles was a great preacher with a unique gift. I went to his "International Pastor's School" conferences at the First Baptist Church of Hammond, Indiana, and was stirred and challenged by it. I usually drove to Hammond, which was about 700 miles. But one time, I flew. I sat by a window, a lady sat in the middle, and another preacher sat on the other side of her. She said, "I feel safe sitting between two preachers. You know the Lord is not going to let this plane go down." I don't know about that, but I'm glad it didn't go down. Dr. Hyles passed away on February 6, 2001, at the age of seventy-four.

Something happened in O'Hare International Airport in Chicago, Illinois, that is a miracle. When I landed, I went to the car rental counter and rented a car. As I was walking down the corridor, I missed my return ticket. I took off back to the rental counter and there, lying on the floor, was my ticket. As busy as O'Hare airport is, no one had picked up my ticket. I went on my way, thanking the Lord, how he had watched out for me. Praise the Lord! The Lord is so good!

Dr. Jack Hyles
Founder of Hyles
Anderson College

In 1986, Ralph Sexton Jr., pastor of the Trinity Baptist Church in Asheville, North Carolina, set up his "Revival" tent in Washington, DC. He called it "Restore the Landmarks." I was blessed to get to attend. I had to get a room on the outskirts of Washington. A friend of mine, who was a former member of Good News Baptist Church, worked for Brother Ralph and was rooming alone. The workers were two in a room, but not Brother Jim Rupe. He said he didn't want anyone to think he was a homosexual. But Brother Jim knew I was staying outside of Washington, and he said, "Come and room with me. I trust you. The room is already paid for." Brother Jim was

Dr. Ralph Sexton Jr.

a man with strong convictions, and, of course, I stayed with him until the end of the meeting. Jim passed away on December 1, 2020, at the age of seventy-nine.

Dr. Tim Lee, who had his legs taken off because of stepping on a mine in Korea, was there to preach. Two men were going to carry him up a set of steep steps to the

Evangelist Dr. Tim Lee

platform. He jumped out of his wheelchair, and up those steps he went. He was a unique preacher. Also, Brother Squire Parson sang in that service.

Brother Ralph's mother, Jaqueline Sexton, was called on to dismiss when the service was over. When she began to pray, the power of God fell. It was probably the most spiritual part of the service. Mrs. Sexton passed away on November 29, 2009, at the age of eighty-four. Ralph Jr.'s father, Ralph Sexton Sr. had passed away on January 13, 2004, at the age of eighty-four.

When I left to go home, I thought the road I was on would run into the interstate toward home. I kept going around and seeing no interstate. Then I realized I was lost. I saw a sign that pointed toward a Naval base. I shot down the exit and came to the security guards. I said, "I'm lost."

They told me how to find my way to the interstate. The lesson here is, I didn't have a map or GPS. I was depending on my sense of direction. Do not think that you know the way to heaven on your own, but pick up the road map; that is the KJV Bible. It will guide you straight through to the throne of God.

I went to the Rock of Ages Conference in Cleveland, Tennessee. Dr. Ed Ballew was the founder and president at that time. They had a big tent with air conditioning in it. That was really nice. I was in service that night, and the next day, I got a call that one of my former members at Zion Hill had died. I told Dr. Ballew I was going to have to leave. He said, "Don't go until you preach. I will call on you to preach before you leave." So that is what he did. I preached that morning before I left. The morning service was in Rev. Bobby Ballew's church instead of under the tent. Rev. Bobby Ballew was Dr. Ed Ballew's brother. I hope that those who were there enjoyed the sermon as much as I did preaching it.

Dr. Ed Ballew with Rev. Sammy Allen

Rev. Sammy Allen preached the Nebo Camp meeting for me at Nebo, North Carolina while I was the moderator. Also, he preached a revival for me at Zion Hill. That is when he encouraged me to come to the Faith Baptist Camp in Resaca, Georgia. Rev. Sammy Allen was the founder and moderator of the camp. My daughter, Sherry, went with me. I had not been there but forty-five minutes when Rev. Allen called on me to preach. That was the first time I had been to the Faith Baptist Camp. I didn't have time to be scared. I had good liberty in preaching. What a privilege to preach in those great places to so many great men.

The first time that I became acquainted with Rev. Sammy Allen was at Camp Zion in Myrtle, Mississippi. I had sat on the same bench he sat on in the back of the tabernacle. Rev. Sammy was very nervous; that was so very obvious as I noticed him on the other end of the pew. Very soon after that Dr. Percy called on him to preach. I call Rev. Sammy the "Walking Bible." He could quote Scriptures faster than you could write them down. Rev. Sammy, in his eighties, could still quote the Word of God. How free-hearted he was that the offerings that he received in revivals he gave to Faith Baptist Camp. Also, when he preached revivals, he would take one of his preacher boys and let them drive. While they were driving, he was reviewing Bible verses. He had a ring with Bible verses and would go around that ring like a Catholic would a prayer rosary, quoting each verse.

Rev. Sammy Allen & me
Rev. Allen is known as
"Walking Bible"

I had Rev. Sammy Allen in two different revivals. One was at Zion Hill and another was at the McDowell Camp Meeting. One night after service at Zion Hill, he wanted me to call Domino's Pizza. When I got them on the line, Brother Sammy talked to the manger. He said to him, "My name is Rev. Sammy Allen, and I am preaching a revival for Rev. Leo Kuykendall here at Zion Hill Baptist Church. I go all over the country preaching revivals, and I use Domino's. Now tell me what can I get a large supreme pizza for?" I was amazed at how much detail Sammy went into to explain to the man who he was. He got a good deal on the pizza!

A Mr. Barnes came from Greenville, South Carolina, to hear Brother Sammy. He did this quite often when Brother Sammy was in revival in the area. After service, Brother Sammy wanted me to get some Breyer's ice cream and bring it to the motel, where he was staying. He told Brother Barnes to help himself to the ice cream. Brother Barnes said, "I am a diabetic." Brother Sammy said, "It is all natural, Brother Barnes; it's all natural. It won't hurt you." He really thought that it wouldn't hurt Brother Barnes to eat it. It was funny the way Brother Sammy said it.

One night in the camp meeting, a church choir was singing. They would sing a song and then talk and then sing another song and then talk. I was sitting beside Brother Sammy, and I said to him, "They are going to take the whole service." Then Brother Sammy jumped up and said to the choir, "Just stand right there, and I will quote a few Scriptures." He preached the whole sermon with them standing there. Brother Sammy could do a service like that, for he could quote so much Scripture. Not many people could do that, but Brother Sammy could. Rev. Sammy Allen passed away on August 2, 2020, at the age of eighty-two.

I heard Dr. Bob Gray preach at Camp Zion the first time that I attended the camp. Dr. Gray pastored Trinity Baptist Church in Jacksonville, Florida. When we went on vacation to Florida, we stopped by Trinity Baptist Church, Dr. Gray would have all the preachers stand and tell where they were from. Dr. Gray called on me to come up to the platform to lead in prayer. The church would seat 1500 to 2000 people. I was scared going up and leading in prayer before that many people. When I got up on the platform, Dr. Gray kept talking for a few minutes. Those few minutes helped me to lose much of that fear. On two different occasions, Dr. Gray called on me to pray. He didn't know me, just that I stood as a preacher. I remember the first sermon that I heard Dr. Gray preach. The title of his

Dr. Bob Gray

sermon was "Paul's Personal Testimony." The sermon lasted for one hour and a half. It was a very powerful sermon! Dr. Gray passed away on November 10, 2007, at the age of eighty-one.

In 1976, I went to the "Sword of the Lord" conference in Atlanta, Georgia. I heard Dr. E. J. Daniels, also known as the "Million Soul Man," Dr. John R. Rice, Dr. Jack Van Impe, also known as the "Walking Bible," and a host of others preach. Dr. E. J. Daniels passed away in 1985 at the age of seventy-eight, and Dr. Jack Van Impe passed away on January 18, 2020, at the age of eighty-eight.

Dr. E. J. Daniels
"Million Soul Man"

Evangelist Dr. Jack Van Impe
Televangelist on end times—rapture

That year, going to the "Sword of the Lord" conference made me late in going back to Gardner Webb College at the outset of the beginning of a new school year. I was going down Highway 221 out of Marion, North Carolina, listening to Evangelist Oliver B. Green on the radio. I was enjoying his preaching and not paying attention to how fast I was going. I looked up and saw a state patrolman. I looked quickly at my speedometer, and I was doing sixty miles per hour in a fifty-five-mile per hour zone. I thought I could get across the hill and maybe hide. But as quickly as he passed me, he immediately turned around and pulled me over. He gave me a speeding ticket. In those days, they would not allow five miles over the speed limit. A ticket ruins a perfectly good day!

Evangelist Jaime Mayorga preached a countywide crusade for me at Zion Hill. I was able to get Jaime into six or seven local schools to preach. This was when you could go into the schools and talk about drugs and addictions but not about God or the Bible. Jaime could get the attention of the students and hold their attention the whole service. On Friday night of the crusade, we advertised the "World's Largest Pizza Blast." What a crowd of young people we had in that service. It was a great crusade.

Jaime Mayorga

I knew three preachers named Larry Brown. As far as I know, they were not related to each other.

The first Larry Brown was a brother to Gary Brown, who drove the bus that threw a rod when we were going to Camp Zion in Myrtle, Mississippi. I had that Larry Brown preach in our Vacation Bible School commencement at Zion Hill. I also preached a revival for him at Flag Pond, Tennessee, and also at Erwin, Tennessee.

Let me add a paragraph right here about Gary Brown's wife Shirley, who was a member of Zion Hill in Marion, North Carolina. She could write shorthand, and she wrote some of my sermons in shorthand. Remember, I was a lot younger then. She said I was preaching at the rate of 180 words per minute. That is moving on. I have slowed down a little since that time.

The second Larry Brown was from Iowa. Shirley Pittman gave me a tape of one of his sermons that he had preached at Eastside Baptist Church in Nebo, North Carolina. As I drove to the pastor's conference in Hammond, Indiana, I listened to the sermon. The sermon was more than an hour long. In one of the services at the conference, I was sitting in the balcony. I introduced myself to the preacher sitting next to me. He, in turn, said, "My name is Rev. Larry Brown from Iowa." I said, "You will not believe this, but I was listening to one of your sermons on tape on the way here." Out of 7,000 preachers in attendance, what would be the chances of that happening? God wanted me to meet Rev. Brown, maybe to be an encouragement to him and to me also.

The third Larry Brown was from North Augusta, Georgia. He was the pastor of Victory Baptist Church. Dr. Larry Brown was a great preacher. He had an unusual style of preaching. He would read his Scripture and then walk down in front of the pulpit and preach all across the front of the church. I had the privilege of going to a hamburger restaurant and eating with him and Rev. Charles Worley. He passed away August 28, 2021 at the age of seventy-four. An outstanding young preacher named Rev. C.T. Townsend became the pastor of Victory Baptist Church. He is a pastor, an evangelist, author, singer, and songwriter. A preacher that God is using mighty.

I was privileged to hear the great Dr. R. G. Lee who was a past president of the Southern Baptist Convention and pastor of Bellevue Baptist Church in Memphis, Tennessee. I heard him preach his classic sermon "Payday Someday" in a Church in West Asheville, North Carolina. That was a hair-raising sermon. Also, I heard him preach at Camp Zion. Dr. Lee passed away on July 20, 1978, at the age of ninety-one.

Dr. R. G. Lee

I heard Dr. John Rawlings, pastor of Landmark Baptist Temple in Cincinnati, Ohio, preach. Dr. Rawlings had a radio program called "The Landmark Hour," which was heard nationwide and into some foreign countries. I heard Dr. Rawlings preach many times on the radio. He had a great voice and was very plain in his preaching. One time, while I was going through Cincinnati, I stopped at his church and went inside to look at the layout of his church. I liked the layout. When I go to churches of great preachers, I always like to stand behind the pulpit to see how it feels. Dr. Rawlings passed away on January 30, 2013, at the age of ninety-nine.

Dr. John Rawlings

I went to New Manna Baptist Church in Marion, North Carolina, to hear Dr. Peter Ruckman. He was the founder of Pensacola Bible Institute in Pensacola, Florida, and pastored Bible Baptist Church in Pensacola. He was born in Wilmington, Delaware. Dr. Ruckman was a preacher, teacher, and a chalk artist. The night I heard him, he had what looked like a four-by-eight-foot chalkboard. He preached on the prodigal son out of the book of Luke chapter 15. He marked off the board into four squares. All the time he was preaching he was drawing. In the first scene, he drew the father and the two sons. In the second scene, he drew a scene in a beer joint and two people sitting at a table with a drink in one hand and a cigarette in the other hand. There was a light hanging over the table, and he made it look smokey like a beer joint. Across from them was a boy and girl sitting on a couch, all hugged up. Then in the third scene, he drew the prodigal son sitting on a stump with his head in his hands and empty beer cans all around him. The fourth scene showed the prodigal son with his head on the bosom of the father, and the father's hand pressed his sons head against his bosom. They were extraordinarily good drawings, and all the time he was preaching, he did not miss a lick. God certainly blessed him with a special talent and great ability.

Dr. Peter Ruckman—Chalk Artist

Vacation in California

Sandra Brittain, my sister Mary Lou, my wife Carolyn, and I went to California on vacation on June 26, 2012–July 10, 2012. We were in San Francisco, down on Fisherman's Warf, a place where tourists go to eat and shop. The ladies went one way, and I went another way. I went into a camera shop. A clerk came up and asked if he could help me. I asked about video equipment. Just then, I looked around and saw several men putting on phylacteries, also known as Tefillin (two small, black leather cubes containing a piece of parchment, inscribed with verses of Deuteronomy 6:4–9, 11:13–21, and Exodus 13:1–16. The boxes are attached with straps, one to the left arm facing the heart and the other to the forehead during weekday morning prayers by Jewish men). I asked him, "Are you Jewish?" He said yes. Then he went further and pointed out a man and said, "That man is the chief rabbi of San Francisco." My heart was thrilled to witness to a rabbi. You must know that I carried a flight bag with tracts and Hebrew New Testaments. The New Testaments are what I received from the founder of "The Hope of Israel Missions," Dr. Daniel Fried, out of Powder Springs, Georgia.

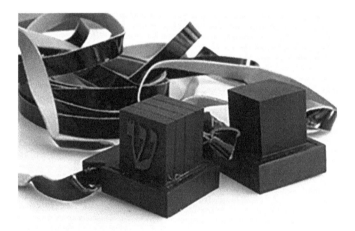

Phylacteries

I tried to give the rabbi a Hebrew New Testament. He refused. Then I tried to give him the Jewish tract "Shalom." He also refused the tract. In our conversation, he said, "You know why they crucified Jesus? It was because he broke the Sabbath." I responded, "No, he was Lord of the Sabbath." I said to the rabbi, "You mean to tell me that you are the chief rabbi of San Francisco, and you have never read the New Testament?" He said, "No, and I've got to go," which ended our conversation. It just got too hot for him.

I do hope he was challenged to purchase a New Testament and read it. I felt that God sent me to California to witness, especially to that rabbi.

I met an Arab Sheik while we were in California. I gave him a tract and witnessed to him about Jesus. He said my Father loved Jesus, and I love Jesus more than my father. Yes, I love Jesus, But Mohammed . . ." I stopped him there and told him that "Jesus is the only way to heaven. Jesus is the Son of God." I told him that he needed to get himself a Scofield KJV Bible. The Muslim people need to read the Bible instead of the Koran.

Arab Sheik I met in California

While in California, I had the privilege to attend Dr. David Jeremiah's church, Shadow Mountain Community Church, in El Cajon, California. We went to the Sunday morning service, and Dr. David Jeremiah preached.

Dr. David Jeremiah & Rev. Leo Kuykendall

Then I went back for the Sunday night service. The ladies did not go. Dr. Tim LaHaye preached that night. I had read some of his books. He had several books on prophecy, one of which was the "Left Behind" series, co-authored by Jerry B. Jenkins. What a thrill it was to hear him in person. I was able to get a picture with both of those great preachers. I had gone to Sea World the day before these pictures were made, and I had a terrible sunburn; that is the reason my face is so red. Dr. LaHaye passed away on July 25, 2016, at the age of ninety-one. He pastored Shadow Mountain Community Church for twenty-five years before Dr. Jeremiah became the senior pastor in 1981.

Me & Dr. Tim LaHaye

Because of flying, I could not take but a few Hebrew New Testaments in the flight bag that I had brought with me. I gave out all my "Five Step" tracts, and I had to call the church and have them mail me more tracts. I remember two distinct times that stand out to me. We were in the farmer's market in Beverly Hills, California. I passed a Jewish girl sitting on a little wall, and I gave her the tract "Shalom." I also gave her my tract that said, "Five Steps to Eternal Life." She said, "This is the one I need." I pray that she got her need met. Also, we were at the Ronald Reagan Library and Museum in Simi Valley, California. The ladies had gone ahead. I was walking up this corridor, and I passed this lady a tract. She looked at it and said "Are you the person whose name is on the tract?" I said "Yes." Most people never ask that. But I did not ask her name. I did ask where she was from because people come there from all over the world. She said she lived in Burbank, California. I believe she must have been a movie star because she was a beautiful woman and had very good manners. I have always wished that I had asked her name. But I hope that the tract spoke to her heart.

Ronald Reagan Library and Museum
Marylou Wilson, Sandra Brittain, Carolyn, & myself

On our vacation to California, we flew first to San Francisco and spent a few nights, then drove down the coastline. We spent a few nights in Hollywood. Then we took a tour of Los Angeles and Beverly Hills. I said, "The hillbillies (us) really did go to Beverly Hills." We went through Universal Studios. Then we drove to San Diego, where we had a meal with my grandson Brittan Nance and his wife Jamilet plus my daughter Sherry, and Doug, who were there on vacation. Sherry and Doug and I went to Sea World, where I got a fierce sunburn. I tell you all of this to let you know that all along the way, I was passing out tracts from San Francisco to San Diego. Are they all effective? I don't know. But our job is to sow the seed and leave the rest to the Lord.

Florida Vacations

In going to Florida on vacation, we went to several different churches: First Baptist Church of Oakland, Florida, Calvary's Chapel in Fort Lauderdale, and Coral Ridge Presbyterian Church in Fort Lauderdale, where Dr. D. James Kennedy was the pastor from 1960 until 2007. Dr. Kennedy was on the WAFG-FM radio station, which he founded, and "The Coral Ridge Hour" TV program, which broadcasts in 200 countries worldwide. He fought liberalism and socialism as hard as any could. One time, I had the privilege of walking out of the Coral Ridge Church with him after service. Walking next to me, I thought that he was smaller than he looked in the pulpit. On September 5, 2007, at the age of seventy-six, Dr. Kennedy went on to that heavenly country. After Dr. Kennedy died, Billy Graham's grandson, Tullian Tchividjian, became the pastor for a year or so. I have heard two of Dr. Graham's grandsons preach. Neither of them had the fire that Dr. Billy Graham had.

Dr. James Kennedy

For many years, we have been going to Florida twice a year on vacation. We go to Fort Lauderdale because there is a big flea market there. People come to that market from all over the world.

Flea market in Fort Lauderdale, Florida

A grand place to pass out tracts and witness. When we first went there, there were a lot of Jewish people there. But today, there are not as many Jews doing business in the flea market. But there are a lot of Jews in South Florida.

**Jew accepting the Hebrew New Testament Bible
at the Florida flea market**

In the last few years, there are more Spanish-speaking folks from South America. When I leave after a week of passing out tracts and witnessing, I feel like I have evangelized many of the countries of South America. Some of us may never go to foreign countries. So, the Lord sends them to us. God, help us to be sensitive of sinners around us. God, help us to be soul-conscious and speak up for Jesus and be a light for Him.

On one occasion, we were in Florida on vacation, and at the motel where we

**Me in a motel
parking lot**

stayed, I ran into a couple from New York. They said that they had never been able to have children. I said, "Let's ask the Lord and see what He says." So, I prayed with them right there outside their motel room. I didn't see them for several years. I wondered if God had answered the prayer that I had prayed. Then a few years later, I saw them again at the same motel. They said, "See the answer to your prayer." They had two boys, very active boys, of which they said, "We want you to be their godfather." The Bible says, "You have not because you ask not."

Another time at the flea market, I lost my checkbook. When I missed it, I went back the way I came and to the vendors that I had talked to. I asked them if anyone found a checkbook. No one had seen it. Remember, this is a flea market with hundreds of people there and many from foreign countries. Someone told me to go to the main office and see if anyone had turned it in. No one had. They took my phone number just in case someone might turn it in. Someone said, "You better call and cancel your checks." This happened on a Saturday.

God is a miracle-working God. About a half-hour to an hour later, I got a call to come to the main office. When I got there, there stood a woman with my checkbook. She had found it and called the number on the checks (which was my home phone number) several times with no answer. So, she took it to the main office. She said, "We are Christians, and so we couldn't keep it." There was four or five hundred dollars in the secret compartment. I said,

"I need to give you some money for turning it in." She said, "No," but I gave her some money anyway. Was that a coincidence, or was God having mercy on us? It was God's good mercy.

Florida vacation photos

Great Experiences

I have been privileged to get to go to some special places. One was the World's Fair in Knoxville, Tennessee on June 18, 1982. Also, I went to Disney World in Orlando, FL. We have been to the space center in Florida several times. We were privileged to see the rocket go off that took the men to the moon. That is the first time they walked on the moon. We were across the bay from where the rocket was launched. Some said it was six miles across, but I can't verify that. I do know that from where we were at, the rocket looked like a big telephone pole. It was while I was watching some of the films at the space center that I realized that space is black. Of course, the Bible bears this out. He talks about "outer darkness" in Matthew 8:12, "But the children of the kingdom shall be cast out into outer darkness: there shall be weeping and gnashing of teeth." Matthew 22:13 says, "Then said the king to the servants, bind him hand and foot, and take him away, and cast him into outer darkness; there shall be weeping and gnashing of teeth." Matthew 25:30 says, "And cast ye the unprofitable servant into outer darkness: there shall be weeping and gnashing of teeth." Outer darkness is beyond all the stars and galaxies. Also, the Bible talks about the "blackness of darkness" in Jude 1:13, "Raging waves of the sea, foaming out their own shame; wandering stars to whom is reserved the blackness of darkness forever." That is where the wicked and ungodly folks will spend eternity.

Me at Cape Canaveral in Florida

We also flew to the island of Hawaii. Things were cheap back then in Hawaii. You could ride the city bus all around the island for twenty-five cents. We went through the Dole Pineapple Plant in Oahu, and I got to drink pineapple juice out of a special spigot. Also, we went to the USS Arizona Memorial, where 1,102 sailors went down with the ship. We toured the National Memorial Cemetery of the Pacific, located at Punchbowl Crater in Honolulu, where 13,000 WWII soldiers and sailors were buried at that time. There are now 53,000 veterans buried in that cemetery (Wikipedia). We saw the Diamond Head volcano that overlooks Honolulu and the Pacific Ocean. Of all the times that I have been to the ocean, the only time that I went in the ocean was in Hawaii. But I went in with my clothes on. I grew up going to a river that ran smoothly. I didn't like to swim in all that motion in the ocean. That was my first time and last time swimming in the ocean. Also, we have been to the Dollywood Theme Park. I asked if Dolly ever came to the park. They said, "Just occasionally." They are well-organized. Dolly lives several miles away at Nashville, and she also goes on tours. This probably explains why she does not show up at Dollywood very often. Of all the great places that I have been and all the great things I have seen, nothing compares to the Holy Land.

Carolyn & me at Dollywood

Me on a ferry while on a cruise

Great people that I have met or (at least) have seen in person.

Carolyn and I attended a special service on Thanksgiving Day in a Methodist Church in Asheville, North Carolina. Billy Graham was preaching in that service. That was the first time that I heard him preach. Then later, I got to attend a Billy Graham crusade in Asheville. I did not get to talk to him, but I did hear him in person. In fact, I went to their counseling meeting, and I was a counselor in that crusade. When Billy Graham had a crusade in Charlotte, I was not able to attend because of eye surgery, but Carolyn and a group from church went. They had a wonderful time. Carolyn said so many people sang in the choir that it reminded her of what heaven would be like.

Evangelist Dr. Billy Graham

Elizabeth Taylor

Another famous person I got to see was Elizabeth Taylor, who was appearing at Belk's Department Store. I wanted to talk to her, but Carolyn and Papaw Edwards didn't want to wait in line. So, I didn't get to speak to her.

Charlie Gibson & Joan Lunde

It was announced that Good Morning America was going to be taping a program at the Biltmore House in Asheville. The first fifty people got in free. I was pastoring Zion Hill in Marion, North Carolina, at that time. I got up early, probably about 4:00 am, to go to Asheville and be there when the gates opened. I got to shake hands with Charlie Gibson and Joan Lunden and see how they taped Good Morning America. Then I got to go through the Biltmore House for free. By the way, Carolyn was born on the Biltmore Estate.

A Time with Rev. Lester Roloff

Dr. Lester Roloff
Pastor of The People's Church

Another time, Rev. Charles Worley called me and said, "Several of us preachers are going to Dr. Roloff's ministry in Corpus Christi, Texas; come and go with us." I said, "I'm going to college, and I have a lot of studying to do." He said, "Take the books with you," and that is what I did. We met his airplane in Statesville, North Carolina and flew to Memphis, Tennessee, where we met Dr. Roloff. He took over the plane, and the other pilot got off. We flew to Garland, Texas, where Dr. Roloff had a meeting with several preachers. He was in a battle with the state of Texas because he would not take a license for his boys' and girls' homes.

Lester Roloff on the steps of his plane

We then flew on to Corpus Christi. When we got off the plane, Dr. Jerry Falwell was waiting to see Dr. Roloff. All of us preachers got to shake hands with Dr. Jerry Falwell. He was another great preacher. He founded the Moral Majority, Faith & Values Coalition, Liberty Council, and Thomas Road Baptist Church, and was the founder and president of Liberty Baptist College, in Lynchburg, Virginia. Jerry Falwell passed away on May 15, 2007, at the age of seventy-three. We were treated like kings while we were at Dr. Roloff's church.

Rev. Jerry Falwell

They had a service at Rev. Roloff's church, The People's Church, that very evening. The singing was already in progress, and Rev. Roloff walked right in and took the microphone as if he had been there from the very start.

The next morning, he had a radio program very early. It was either 6:00 or 7:00 am. So, he had all of us say a few words on his broadcast, "The Family Altar." Then he took us to his house for breakfast; they called him a health fanatic. He did not drink anything with his meals, but one of his men snuck us some orange juice while Dr. Roloff was in another room.

Lester Roloff in the studio, where we spoke on the radio program

Dr. Roloff told one of his pilots to take us down to "The Lighthouse for Boys," which was out in the Gulf of Mexico. It was far enough out until you had to fly or take a boat. When we got close to the lighthouse, there were some boys on the dock, and he took a dive down toward it. In other words, he buzzed them. Some of the boys on the dock dove into the water. Then he landed on the beach, and some of the boys came with a boat to take us up a canal to the lighthouse. The boys at the lighthouse were either in trouble or taken out of prisons and put out there in the middle of the Gulf. All they did was fish and have preaching and singing. We had a service with them, and all of us were given a chance to say a few words. I talked to one of the boys, and he said this particular pilot always buzzed them coming in and going out. I was dreading going back to the mainland. So, when he took off, one of the men had left his safety belt hanging out of the door. The pilot would not let him open the door to pull it in. The pilot landed on the beach again so he could pull the safety belt in. The pilot took off again, flying way high, and I said, "Well, he's not going to buzz them this time." Low and behold, he swung around, and down we went. I thought I was just going to enjoy the ride; if we crash, we'd just crash. So, I enjoyed the buzz.

We flew with Dr. Roloff to Hattiesburg, Mississippi, where he had a girl's home called the Rebekah Home. All those girls did at that home was farm and memorize Scripture. One girl had memorized Psalm 119. That psalm has 176 verses. What a memory. We had a service there with those girls before we left.

After that meeting, we flew back to North Carolina and went to Landis Baptist Church in Landis, North Carolina. Dr. Roloff preached that night. As we were flying back and got over North Carolina, Rev. Charles Worley said that his radio program was on the air. So, it was tuned in. It came in loud and clear at an altitude of about 15,000 or 20,000 feet. I thought of the Scripture Habakkuk 2:14, "For the earth shall be filled with the knowledge of the glory of the Lord as the waters cover the sea." In those two days, we were in six services. It was a great experience being with such a great soldier of the cross, and thanks to Rev. Charles Worley for inviting me. His church supported Dr. Roloff, but our church did not. One preacher who was supposed to go couldn't go, so that left an opening for me. Thank You, Lord! Rev. Charles Worley passed away June 19, 2022 at the age of eighty-one years old.

Dr. Roloff had a plane crash with the very plane we flew down there and back in. It took his life on November 4, 1982, and four others on the plane died with him. He was sixty-eight years old. They still play his tapes on the radio. He had such a clear sounding voice to preach and to sing with. He was an unusual man. You can hear many of his songs on a link from Dr. Phil Kids' website, and on www.jesus-is-savior.com.

I was privileged to hear LtCol Oliver North at the country club in Gastonia, NC. He was running for the United States Senate as the republican candidate for the state of Virginia. The year was 1994. When he finished his powerful presentation, I told him. "You should not be running for the Senate, but you ought to be running for the president of the United States." Also, I heard him speak at the First Baptist Church of Indian Trail, NC. I enjoyed his presentations on both occasions.

Jewish Mission

Carolyn put her name in one of those contests, where you could win four days and three nights at a resort in Miami, Florida. Of course, everybody who entered won. So, they put us on a bus and took us across the Everglades to Lehigh, where they were selling empty lots to build on. The salesman turned the pressure on. I told him that I was a preacher, and he said, "We will give you a lot (there) to build a church on." With all the pressure, we said yes to buying a lot. The salesman said we had thirty days to cancel. When we returned home, I called and canceled the sell. On the bus ride back across the Everglades, I sat across the aisle from a Jewish lady. I asked her what she thought about Jesus. She said, "He was a prophet. But, he was crazy because He went out into the wilderness and almost starved himself to death." That was my first encounter with a Jew, but there were many more to come. "To the Jew first" (Rom. 1:16, 2:9–10). In witnessing to the Jews, I asked them if they knew what they have given to the world. They do not know. I tell them what the Jews have given to the world:

1. The knowledge of one God;
2. The Scriptures (the Bible); and
3. A Savior (Jesus Christ).

To the Church world, I say don't ever forget that the Jews gave us those three things.

Later, Carolyn and I purchased a time share in Florida, which is a bad thing. But the Lord used it to open a mission field for me to witness to the Jews. As I began to witness to a few Jews, I recognized that most of them knew nothing about the Bible. They are taught by their rabbis not to believe in Jesus Christ. I was witnessing to this one Jewish girl, and I mentioned Billy Graham. She did not know who he was. I thought everyone in the United States knew him or knew about him. Further, I soon realized that she didn't know much about the Bible or Jesus Christ.

As we were going home, the Lord put on my heart to write a tract for the Jews. My first draft, I entitled "Dear Jewish Friend." By that title, they recognized that I was a Gentile. Then I changed the title to "Shalom" and put the Star of David on the front cover. Many will not take one, but many are glad to get one, plus a Hebrew copy of the New Testament, which I obtain from Dr. Daniel Freid, founder of the Hope of Israel Mission Board in Powder Springs, Georgia.

Dr. Daniel Freid
Founder of Hope of Israel Mission Board

I was in Hollywood, Florida, and went into a shop, which was owned by a Jewish man. I began to talk to him about Jesus. He said, "I am like my rabbi, who said when the Messiah comes, I am going to ask Him how many times has He been here. He will say only once, and that is right now." I said, "I'm sorry, but the Bible says in Zechariah 13:6, 'One will say unto Him, what are these wounds in Thine hands? Then He shall answer, those with which I was wounded in the house of my friends.' Also, Isaiah 53:5 says, 'But He was wounded for our transgressions.'" The proof that Jesus was the Messiah and died on Calvary will be the wounds in His hands. Read John 20:26–29.

I met an older gentleman on a bench in a JC Penney store in Florida. I tried to give him the tract, "5 Steps to Eternal Life," and he replied, "I am Jewish." I said, "I've got something for you." I gave him the tract "Shalom." He began to read. I was impressed with the speed that he was able to read the tract. He had told me that:

1. He was in pain all the time;
2. That he was dying; and
3. And he asked me to pray for him.

When I got back to Zion, I asked the church to pray for him.

I was back in Florida six months later, to the same store, and the same bench. There was the same man. He said, "Your prayers didn't work," but they did, for he was still alive. I asked him if he had read the tract. He said, "Yes, but I couldn't understand it." He had bought some children's Bible story books. He said that he could understand them better. In the meantime, I had changed several things in the tract because of questions he asked before, and so I gave him a revised tract. I told him, "Read it and do what it said." I was back there six months later. No sign of him. Another six months later I was there again, and still no sign of him.

I saw two Jewish ladies and asked about him. They told me that he had died. That he had been editor of the Fort Lauderdale Gazette newspaper. Then I understood why he could read so fast. I believe that he must have gotten saved because of divine providence. He was eighty years old. What are the chances of going to the same store and the same bench and find the same man there six months later. For that reason, I hope to meet him in heaven.

**Me in Florida with
Bibles & tracts in my flight bag**

I gave another Jewish lady, Randi, a Jewish tract, plus a Hebrew New Testament. She said her family was not religious. She was happy to get the Hebrew New Testament. I told her she could hear some of my sermons on YouTube. She had a Christian lady who was a good influence on her. She told me later that I had saved her life because now she knew Jesus was the Savior and that He was the Messiah. She said, "There is no coincidence that I met you and that you walked through our doors here and shared the Hebrew New Testament and the Shalom tract. I have never felt more gratitude and love for God's mercy and Jesus's love. You changed my life. Thank you! Your literature and our conversations have drawn me closer and closer to God and Jesus Christ." What a blessing to reach some of the Jewish people for Jesus! Randi is on fire for the Lord. She has a great testimony, and the Lord is using her in witnessing to other people.

Randi
Jewish lady I met in Florida

We were in the big Sawgrass Mills Mall. I met a young rabbi. I would say in his twenties or thirties from Hollywood, Florida. He had four or five young children. I tried to give him the Hebrew New Testament. He looked at it, then handed it back to me. I said, "Take it and read it," but he refused.

Carolyn was in line to pay for what she wanted to buy. It was a long line, and she has a hard time standing. I went over and told her that I would stand in line for her. About that time, the line moved up, and behind her was a young lady. So, I gave her the "5 Steps" tract and asked here where she was from. She said, "Where do you think?" I had just given a girl from Colombia a track. This girl looked like her, and I said, "Colombia." She said, "I am from Israel." I said, "I got something for you," and I gave her the Hebrew New Testament. She was so happy to get it. As I walked away, I heard the rabbi hollering at her. I hope that she got to keep the Bible. The rabbis are in prison because they are afraid to mention the name Jesus, the only name whereby you can be saved. Acts 4:12 says, "Neither is there salvation in any other: for there is none other name under heaven given among men, whereby we must be saved." In John 8:24, Jesus said, "I said therefore unto you, that ye shall die in your sins: for if ye believe not that I am he, ye shall die in your sins." John 8:32 says, "And ye shall know the truth, and the truth shall make you free." John 8:36 says, "If the Son, therefore shall make you free, ye shall be free indeed." Jesus will set you free if you will believe and trust him. Further, they want all the Jewish people to be in prison by never mentioning the name Jesus.

I gave one Jewish man a copy of the Hebrew New Testament in the flea market. He was so happy he wanted to pay for it. I told him it was free. But in spite of that, he gave me a book off his table of books that he had for sale. I told him, "You don't have to do that; it is free." He insisted and gave me a book on the Twin Towers, of which it had a lot of facts about them. He was so thrilled to get the Bible which he thought he had to pay for.

Man from Montenegro
I met him at the motel in Florida in November 2020

By the way, I have given out many Jewish tracts and Hebrew New Testaments. Many are excited to get them, and others refuse to take them. Pray for the salvation of the Jewish people. Remember, "To the Jew first" Romans 1:16.

Holy Land Experiences

First trip to the Holy Land
March 1971
I am on the top row—sixth from right, wearing a tan hat.

I have had wonderful experiences in going to the Holy Land five different times: October 18, 1971, March 13, 1973, March 10, 1979, March 1, 1977, and March 10, 1980. The first time, Good News Baptist Church made up enough money to send me. Brother Gerald Payne gave one hundred dollars on my trip. He and I roomed together also. He was a dear friend. The first time I went to the Holy Land, we flew with Swiss Air. We flew on a 747 plane. It held 462 people and their luggage. That was what I was told. It would leave the ground in forty-five seconds, a powerful plane. We were to land in Geneve and Zurich, Switzerland, before we got to Israel. As we flew over the Swiss Alps, we could see the mountains sticking up above the clouds, and then the plane began to descend into the clouds and the mountaintops sticking above the clouds. I said, "I hope the pilot knows where he is going." When we came under the cloud ceiling, we were very high. That is how high the Swiss Alps are.

Rev. Charles Worley and Rev. Bill Worley were in our group. Rev. Charles wanted to be baptized in the river of Jordan. Rev. Richard Horn said, "Hey, you just can't do that without a church authorizing it." We had five members from Good News in the group, so we voted to take Rev. Charles in as one of our members and to baptize him. So, I had the privilege of baptizing him in the Jordan River. I have kidded Rev. Charles on the fact that he never did pay his tithes to our church. That was a great tour, and it was an all-Israel tour.

On most of the tours in the Holy Land, the bus drivers and the tour guides were Arabs. On this particular tour, the guide was a Jew. One particular night, we spent the night on a kibbutz (agricultural village). While there, we had a service that night. The next morning when we went to the bus, the Jewish guide said to another preacher and to me, "What if the Jewish people had received Jesus as their Messiah, what about the blood theory?" The other preacher was stumbling around, trying to answer him. I was trying to think what would have happened if they had. accepted Him as their Messiah. Of course, the Lord knew they would not receive Him. Read Isaiah 53:1–12. I said, "If they had received Him, He still would have died and then been resurrected and set up His kingdom right then. The Bible said in Matthew 20:28, "Even as the Son of man came not to be ministered unto, but to minister and to give His life a ransom for many." He came to die for the sins of the world. When I gave him that answer, he seemed to be satisfied. I have never heard from him since that tour. We called him "Jeff the Jew." The people on that tour prayed for his salvation.

On other times that I went to the Holy Land, we went to other countries. One was Egypt. It was one of the longest flights from New York to Cairo, Egypt; it was fourteen hours. That's a long time to be on an airplane.

While in Egypt, we went up inside one of the pyramids, rode on camels, took a boat ride on the Nile River, saw the Sphinx, and traveled the streets of Cairo. Those people could not drive if they did not have a horn. They would wake us up in the morning with all the horns blowing.

One time, we landed in Rome. While in Rome, we took a tour of the Vatican; we went in to St. Peter's Square, and we saw the statue of St. Peter. Also, we saw the Trevi Fountain and the Coliseum, where many saints and Christians were killed and eaten by lions. Further, we got to go down and see the catacombs, where many Christians hid from their persecutors, and many were buried there.

One time, we landed in Paris, France. We didn't get to take a tour there; we were supposed to, but because our flight had been late, we didn't get to. I was dumbfounded to see their restrooms. They were open. You could see people using the urinals.

We also landed in Athens, Greece. We did not get to take a tour there either. Again, we landed in Holland because some little thing was wrong with the plane. One time, we landed on the Island of Cyprus.

The first time we went to the Holy Land, and we flew out of Asheville, North Carolina, to New York. We had to wait until about 7:00 pm to fly to the Holy Land. While waiting in the airport, I passed out some tracts. This one fellow had these expensive-looking cowboy boots on. I gave him a tract. When I sat back down with my group, they asked, "Do you know who that was?" I said, "No." They said, "That is Jimmy Dean, the sausage man." I said, "He needs the gospel too." The gospel is for the whole world, the rich, the poor, the educated and uneducated, and the famous and the unknown. Jimmy Dean died on June 13, 2010. I hope that he was saved when he died.

Jimmy Dean

One time that we were all set to go to the Holy Land, Mrs. Hensley, one of our members, came to the parsonage and began to beg us not to go. She said she was afraid something would happen to us. We could not back out; everything was set to go. Our first stop was to land in Amman, Jordan. We were in the clouds, and the pilot kept turning one way and then another. I began to think what Mrs. Hensley said would come to pass. It was snowing in Amman, and the pilot could not land, so he took us on to Damascus, Syria, which was only thirty minutes in flight time. The Arabs there did not like Americans at that time. Finally, a bus was found to take us back to Amman. It took eight hours on that bus with no heat, and it was cold. The driver was angry. I am not sure if it was because he didn't want to make the trip or because we were Americans. Someone had some candy, and I got some and gave it to him. Then he turned sweet. The old saying, "you can catch more flies with a spoonful of honey than you can with a barrel of vinegar," is certainly true.

While in the country of Jordan, we were taken down to Petra, which was a real experience. Many believe, and I believe also that it is the place prepared for Israel (the woman of Revelation chapter 12) during the great tribulation.

Most everybody has heard about a mirage. I saw several mirages on the drive through the desert going to Petra. It is like "Fool's Gold." It looks like water, but there is nothing there. The devil fools a lot of people with his mirages. Don't be deceived by the devil; he is the master deceiver. All you have to do to go to hell is be deceived on how you get saved. Read God's Word; it will show you the truth.

As we were crossing from Jordan into Israel at the Allenby Bridge, now also known as the King Hussein Bridge, I had a shopping bag full of tracts. One of the preachers on the trip preached me a sermon because of the tracts. He said, "You are going to get the whole group held up, and they may put you in jail." He really gave me a rebuking for having all those tracts. What could I say? I had them, and I was not going to throw them away. When we went through the checkpoint, I set the shopping bag of tracts on the counter. The Israeli soldiers opened it up and closed it again and pushed it on through. Not one word was mentioned about them. What God is in, He will bless. If every Christian who went to the Holy Land would pass out tracts and witness, the Jewish people would be evangelized.

Allenby Bridge or King Hussein Bridge

Allenby Bridge or King Hussein Bridge
Tour Bus crossing with soldier on the bridge

I remember another time riding in the back seat of the bus, and I would put a tract out the window every so often, about every two or three minutes. I figured someone would find it, read it, and maybe get saved. The bus driver surely saw the tracts flying out the window, but he never said anything to me.

How wonderful it is to go to the sites that you have read about in the Bible, such as a boat ride across the Sea of Galilee, go to Capernaum, where Jesus lived, to

Nazareth, were Jesus grew up, and to Bethlehem, where Jesus was born. We went to the head waters of the Jordan River, which is called Caesarea Philippi, where Jordan flows out of the mountain. The mountain springs that I was familiar with were just a small stream. But the Jordan coming out of that mountain must have been twenty feet to forty feet wide. It was a most beautiful sight.

Further, we went down to Jericho and the Dead Sea, then up to Masada, the ancient fortress that overlooks the Dead Sea. It was the place where the Jews took their last stand when the Romans destroyed Jerusalem. It is an amazing place. Then we went up to Jerusalem. We walked the streets of old Jerusalem and went to the Garden Tomb. We were able to go up on Calvary three different times. Not many people get to do that. Then we went to the Temple Mount, where you have to pull your shoes off to go into the Dome of the Rock Mosque.

Dome of the Rock Mosque (photo by David Baum)

On my first trip to the Holy Land, I had bought a pair of new shoes to wear on my trip. You don't want to do that. My feet were hurting. We were doing a lot of walking. When we came out, Brother Gerald Payne said, "Leo, this is your chance to pick you out a pair of shoes." He said this because there were all kinds of shoes sitting there. He was only kidding. Brother Payne passed away on June 20, 2017, at the age of eighty.

Gerald Payne

We went to the Wailing Wall, where the Jews go to pray, and there is a place next to the wall that the Jews would go in and put the phylacteries on. There were several young people being taught what to do. I thought, *If I started preaching "Jesus" in here, they would have stoned me or thrown me in jail. But when Elijah comes, many will believe him and be converted.* What a great experience and what enlightenment that I received in taking these trips to the Holy Land.

Wailing Wall

Home Remedies, Vitamins & Herbs

My mother doctored us with a lot of home remedies. She hardly ever took us to the doctor. I remember one time, my brothers were over in the woods cutting down trees and then cutting them up. The cows started coming around, eating the leaves off the cut trees. They told me to run them off; I was barefoot. I was running them off when I hooked my big toe over a double-bitted ax that was under the leaves, and laid it open. My brother picked me up and carried me to the house. Mama put kerosene on the cut and wrapped it up. No doctor, no stitches. That was the way many people did back in those days. But my toe got better. There is an old saying that says, "What you don't know won't hurt you." But that is not true. I didn't know the ax was under the leaves, and it did hurt me. Many things will hurt you that you don't know. That is the reason you need Jesus in your heart and to read the Bible, God's Word, to let you see the unknown. By the way, you probably couldn't use kerosene today for cuts because of the additives that have been added.

When I was very young, I had earaches a lot. Mama would put a flat iron on the stove and get it warm, not real hot, and then wrap a towel around it. She would put a little sweet oil in my ear and then put the wrapped flat iron against my ear. That felt so good. My ear would pop and crack, but it got better.

When I would get a chest cold, Mama made an onion polis or mustard polis and put it on my chest. I didn't like either one. But they worked.

Some of those old-fashioned remedies work as well as modern medicine.

Years ago, I subscribed to Prevention Magazine. In those days, it was a good magazine. I learned a lot about vitamins, things that are good for people to know about how to maintain good health. Salvation is of the Lord, safety is of the Lord, health is of the Lord, and healing is of the Lord. Doctors may operate and give you medicine, but when it is all said and done, it is the Lord who heals and lets you get better.

A missing link in my knowledge was herbs. I heard a presentation by an Indian called "Chief Two Trees." He talked about vitamins and herbs. I had never thought much about herbs until that time. I bought a book on herbs by Maria Treben, called "Health Through God's Pharmacy." Of all the books I have about vitamins and herbs, I enjoy her book above them all. Carolyn calls me "Chief Three Trees" because I tell people about certain vitamins and herbs. In her book, Maria Treben talks about Swedish bitters. When I got to where I couldn't remember people's names, I would take a few days of Swedish bitters, and it was like flushing the cobwebs out of my brain. But I will have to say that they have cut back on the herbs in them. They are not as good as they use to be.

Here are a few things that I have tried:

Black strap molasses worked to bring up my wife's platelets.

Lysine is good for fever blisters and shingles.

Acidophilus is good for halitosis and ulcers in your mouth.

Burdock root is good for keeping you from getting boils.

Aspirin is a pain killer and inflammation fighter but also blood thinner. Not everyone can take aspirins.

Siberian ginseng may keep your hair from falling out.

Epsom salt or either table salt is good to soak your feet in for sores.

Coffee is good to stimulate your brain. For example:

I was driving to Duke Hospital to see a lady named Angel. This was about a two or two-and-a-half-hour drive. I was trying to memorize a Scripture out of Philippians. I couldn't seem to get every verse memorized all the way through. I heard this girl talking about how coffee would stimulate your brain. I was never a coffee drinker before. But on this particular day, I was headed back to Duke Hospital, and I drank a cup of coffee before I started. You won't believe this, but I memorized that Scripture with ease. They say coffee also helps ward off Alzheimer's. That is worth you trying it.

Lonnie Hatherly asked me to go with him to pick blueberries. We went to a place called "Shining Rock" in the Pisgah National Forest. I drove my 1951 Chevrolet. Shining Rock was about nine miles off the main road. We got there about four o'clock in the afternoon. We picked blueberries until supper time. Lonnie cooked fatback and Vienna sausages. From that meal, I got sick as a dog. I rolled around the back seat of my car all night and vomited several times. The next morning, I told him that I was going to have to go home. He said there were other people picking blueberries that he could get a ride home with, so I left. There was a spout of water on the side of the road, where people could get a drink of cold mountain water. This was on the way coming down the mountain. I stopped and got a drink of water, but I vomited it up. When I got home, Dad and Mama had gone shopping, so I went to bed for a while. When I got up, I asked my Aunt Zora, who lived with us, to cook me an Irish potato. I told her not to put anything in it; no butter, no salt, nothing. I was able to keep it down. You might try that when you are sick at your stomach.

Mama, me, and Aunt Zora

When it comes to my health, I have had good health most of my life. I have had some back problems in the past. I remember going to the chiropractor, and I could hardly lie down on his table or even get up. Further, I remember a time that I would drive my Honda to the hospital. For some reason, it threw my back in a strain. When I tried to get out of the Honda, I had to pull myself out with a lot of pain. I would stand there for a minute or two, then the pain went away, and I could walk like there was nothing wrong. I thought if someone was watching me, they probably would say, "What is wrong with that fellow? He's acting very strange."

I've had two hernia surgeries, gallbladder surgery, and, of course, my tonsils taken out. In 2017, I had pneumonia, and the virus went to my heart, which is called a-fib. I started smothering. I went to the doctor, and he put me straight in the hospital. I thought that my time had come, but the Lord spared me. They sent me home from the hospital too early. I started to smother again. So, Denise called the members on the "One Call" and told them to pray for me. God heard their prayers, and I stopped smothering. Thank you, Lord, for your mercy!

A few months after being in the hospital, I had to have a pacemaker-defibrillator put in on December 13, 2017. I have asked the doctor, "How do you know when it kicks in?" He said, "You will know it because it will be like a mule kicking you in the chest." I said, "Then it has never kicked in." The doctor said, "That is good." God is so good!

Healing

A lot of people do not believe in the supernatural power of God. But I do. The Lord has touched me on several different occasions. One time, I had a cyst come up in my eye. I could look in the mirror and see it. I could feel it with my finger. I went to the doctor. He told me, "I would have to get it cut out; it will never go away." When I got home, I told my sister Mary Lou about what he said. She responded, "Why don't you believe the Lord to take care of it?" Thus, I called and canceled the surgery that had already been scheduled. After that, I forgot about the cyst. One day, I looked in the mirror, and it was gone. I felt to see, and there was no cyst there. The Lord does heal!

Another time, I had gone to the doctor about a problem. He said, "You need surgery." I said, "Doc, I'm sorry to tell you that I haven't prayed about this problem like I should." I did pray about it, and it has been probably thirty years since that time and no surgery. Thank you, Lord!

On two different occasions, the Lord touched my voice to let me preach revivals. One Sunday morning, a preacher called me and said, "I want you to preach a revival for me." I said, "When?" He said, "Tomorrow night." I said, "I am so hoarse that I can hardly talk." He said, "If you don't, I will have to preach it myself." I said, "I will come and try. If I can't, then you will have to preach it yourself." On that Sunday morning, I had a missionary from Guatemala, Rev. Willard Rowe, to preach for me. He was one of Zion Hill's missionaries. He told me about eucalyptus that helped him. Further, he said, "Halls cough drops have eucalyptus in them." So, I bought some Halls and ate them, two at a time. I went and preached that revival with no problem. In fact, it was a great revival. Sometimes the Lord uses a means to an end. Isaiah 38:21 says, "Let them take a lump of figs, and lay it for a plaster upon the boil, and he shall recover."

Another time, I was to preach a revival at Rev. Bobby Jewel's church in Indiana. I was so hoarse I could hardly preach. I was the pastor of Zion Hill at that time. So, on that Sunday night, before Monday when I was to preach for Rev. Jewel, I went to the altar and asked the church to pray for me. One of the brothers laid his hand on my head and prayed. Of course, the church gathered around and also prayed. I went to Indiana and preached that revival with no problem. As the song goes, "Jesus on the main line, tell him what you want" because he is listening, and he has the power to answer any and every prayer. These are not the only times the Lord has touched me. I want to acknowledge his goodness and love toward me.

There was a time that I was having back pain. It didn't bother me through the day, but when I went to bed, my back would give me pain when I would turn over. Then it began to give me pain through the day. So, I began to ask the Lord to heal me, which He didn't see fit to do right then. One day as I was praying, I said, "Lord, why won't you heal me?" The answer came back immediately. The Lord said, "What about those books you borrowed and haven't taken back? What about the books you get every month that you aren't sure you have paid for all of them? I said, "Calf rope, Lord." (I surrender; I'll take care of these matters). The Lord healed me immediately. Thank God for the correcting of the Lord! Hebrews 12:5–11:

"And ye have forgotten the exhortation which speaketh unto you as unto children, my son, despise not thou the chastening of the Lord, nor faint when thou are rebuked of him: For who the Lord loveth He chasteneth, and scourgeth every son whom He receiveth. If ye endure chastening, God dealeth with you as with sons; for what son is he whom the Father chasteneth not? But if ye be without chastisement, whereof all are partakers, then are ye bastards, and not sons. Furthermore, we have had fathers of our flesh which corrected us, and we gave them reverence: shall we not much rather be in subjection unto the Father of Spirits, and live? For they verily for a few days chastened us after their own pleasure; but He for our profit, that we might be partakers of His holiness.

Now no chastening for the present seemeth to be joyous, but grievous: nevertheless, afterward it yieldeth the peaceable fruit of righteousness unto them which are exercised thereby. "

Chastisement certainly is not joyous, but thank God for it. It puts us back on track. Thank you, Lord, for chastisement.

When Carolyn's sister, Sandy Whitaker, was in the hospital, at the point of death, her daughter Karen was sitting by her bed. The chaplain came in and asked if he could have a word of prayer with her mother. Karen told him no, "Uncle Leo had it under control. He has a direct line to God. He's got it covered." Well, in a sense, that is true of every Christian. It sure is a blessing for someone to have that much confidence in you. God help us all to live a life so that people know we have been with Jesus. Acts 4:13 says, "and they took knowledge of them, that they had been with Jesus." Thank God, Sandy did get better and is still kicking.

Visitation

As a pastor, I have always believed in visitation; visiting hospitals, nursing homes, shut-ins, the sick, and knocking on doors—soul-winning.

The Lord gave me training in that field. My brother Delmar would buy truckloads of apples or peaches or watermelons or cantaloupes or green beans to peddle them out through the community. Guess who had to run to the door to ask if they wanted to buy whatever he had at that time? It was me knocking on doors.

Then, when I went to work at the telephone company, I was an installer-repair man. That is where you go from house to house, job to job. So that took me to a lot of different homes to install and work on their telephone. That was knocking on doors.

When I became a pastor, I still had to keep on knocking on doors. It is our responsibility as pastors and as Christians to evangelize. Paul went "from house to house" (Acts 20:20). And so should we.

A man told me that he lived right across the road in front of a church, and nobody had ever knocked on his door and invited him to church. Nobody had ever visited him to ask him if he was saved. How sad. What will the Lord say to that church when they stand before Him? If you have never heard the song, "In the shadow of the Cross," you need to get a copy and listen to it. A lady sang that song in a revival that I preached. When I was given the pulpit, I said to the congregation, "Maybe we should just dismiss and go out and knock on doors." This song talks about an old man who died and had never been to church. When they went to his house, on his body fell the shadow of the cross from the steeple of the church next door.

Just before I left Good News Baptist Church, I visited Winfred Bennett. Years came and went. One day, many years after Good News, as I was working on my house in Candler, North Carolina, a truck pulled up, and Winfred Bennett got out. He told me that after I visited him, he got back in church and surrendered to preach. He pastored Harmony Grove Baptist Church in Canton, North Carolina, for thirty-nine years. Rev. Winfred had bought George and Carrie Davis' house just above my property. Rev. Bennett's last sermon was a Father's Day message. Rev. Bennett passed away on July 9, 2020, at the age of seventy-seven. Visitation does pay.

When I came to Zion in Gastonia, I visited one of the shut-in members named Mrs. Leeora Dockery. What was so amazing about this lady was she had copied the Bible through, in long hand, twice. She was seventy-eight years old at that time I visited her. It is hard to imagine how long it took and how hard that would be! Mrs. Dockery passed away on March 18, 1999, at the age of eighty-three.

I have had some great experiences visiting and, of course, I have had a few doors slammed in my face. One great experience was when I visited Eloise Johnson. She had lived a rough life, as many have said. I went back to visit Eloise several times. She told my wife that she knew the preacher wouldn't come by, and low and behold, he caught me drinking. Finally, she came to church and got saved. Eloise brought her neighbor, Juanita Edwards, who got saved, and she and Eloise joined Zion and were baptized on May 25, 1997. Eloise then got her daughter, Diane Harding, and her husband "Ace" Harding, also Linda Self, Linda's brother-in-law, James Self Jr., and her granddaughter

Robin Sanders. Carolyn thought Eloise got her son, Wayne Sanders, in church, but Wayne told Carolyn, "No, it was the preacher. Eloise did get Wayne's sister-in-law, Savannah Lanier, and husband Jack, and some of her other grandchildren in church. That is the way it is supposed to work, like a domino effect.

Eloise Johnson

Eloise passed away on January 7, 2008, at the age of eighty-three. Her neighbor, Juanita Edwards, passed away on April 18, 2001, at the age of fifty-nine.

The following information is put in to let you see how a family is sometimes affected and how important it is to be in church and be committed to Christ.

Eloise's son, Wayne Sanders, joined Zion on April 2, 2006, and passed away on December 24, 2011, at the age of sixty-six.

Eloise's granddaughter, Robin, joined on March 13, 2006, and passed away on May 3, 2019, at the age of forty-nine.

Eloise's grandson, Steven Sanders Sr., passed away on November 15, 2010, at the age of forty-three.

Eloise's great-great granddaughter, Ava Sanders, passed away on November 22, 2012, at the age of three months.

Her daughter, Linda Self, kept coming to church after her mother passed in 2008. She did not join until June 26, 2011, and passed away on July 31, 2011, at the age of sixty-four.

Linda's son, Terry Self, visited when Eloise passed. He lived in Tampa, Florida. He passed away on March 7, 2008, at the age of forty-three.

Linda's son, Bobby Eugene Self, passed away on July 22, 2000, at the age of thirty-one.

Eloise's daughter, Diane Harding, joined on December 7, 2003, and passed away on July 16, 2017, at the age of sixty-seven.

Diane's husband, "Ace," joined on March 5, 2006, and passed away on August 5, 2008, at the age of fifty-six.

There have been five generations of Eloise's family that attended Zion Baptist Church, and I have buried four generations of them. Life is so short; prepare to meet God now.

Ecclesiastes 12:1
"Remember **now** thy Creator in the days of thy youth, while the evil days cone not, nor the years draw nigh, when thou shalt say, I have no pleasure in them" (emphasis mine).

2 Corinthians 6:2
"Behold, **now** is the accepted time; behold **now** is the day of salvation" (emphasis mine).

Isaiah 1:18
"Come **now**, and let us reason together, saith the Lord: though your sins be as scarlet, they shall be as white as snow; though they be red like crimson, they shall be as wool" (emphasis mine).

Another time, I was visiting on a Thursday night in a housing division. Brother Bobby Cleveland and Allen Costner were with me. They went down one side of the street, and I went down the other side of the street. I went up to knock on the door of this house, and lo and behold, there lay a five-dollar bill on the porch. What is so amazing about this was that the wind was blowing very strong. But it didn't blow away. I could not understand. I knocked on the door, and the man of the house answered the door. I introduced myself and invited him to church. I said, "If you will come to church, I will give you five dollars." The man said, "You don't have to do that." Of course, I was kidding him. I told him that I found the five-dollar bill lying on his porch. I do not know why this happened the way it did, for the man never came to church that I know of unless he read the tract that I gave him and either started attending another church or possibly got saved. But I will find out when I get to heaven.

I went to the VA hospital in Oteen, North Carolina, to visit a patient. This was a family member of one of our church members. He was in a room, where they had four beds with patients. I gave him the plan of salvation and prayed with him. I asked him, "Did you asked the Lord to save you?" He replied, "No." I told him, "You will have to ask him." I prayed again. His answer was the same. Then I went to the other men in the room. One was a Black man. I asked him, "Are you saved?" He said, "I wasn't until I heard you tell him what to do, and I asked the Lord to save me, and now

I am saved." That is what is called an indirect witness. Many times, the Lord uses an indirect witness to win others.

One of our deacons, Billy Poteat, at Zion Hill, was saved the same way. A preacher came to witness to his dad. Billy was a small boy and was down behind the couch. The Preacher told his dad how to be saved, but his dad didn't get saved, but Billy did behind the couch. So indirect witnessing, many times, brings forth great fruit. Billy is now a pastor.

Front row: Billy & Regina Poteat
Back row: Matthew & Andrew Poteat

Counseling with different individuals over the years, I probably saved the lives of at least two men and possibly a third, and I hope many others, through preaching the Word of God. I had two men come to me for counsel with the intent to kill another person. I explained to them that the Bible says in Exodus 20:13, "Thou shalt not kill," and they would have blood on their hands, and they would be put in prison if they followed through with their plans and, thank God, they took my advice.

I visited another man in the hospital who told me when he got out of the hospital, he was going to kill his neighbor. His neighbor had put a fence up just about a foot over on this man's property. I told him it's not worth getting blood on your hands and that he would send that neighbor to hell, and he would be put in jail. It turns out that this man did not kill his neighbor, and he did not live very long after that. First John 3:15 says, "Whosoever hateth his brother is a murderer: and ye know that no murderer hath eternal life abiding in him."

Many today do not care what the Bible says about murder. But I say to any and all who read these lines, it is not worth violating the Word of God and stand before God with blood on your hands. In fact, God has never retracted Genesis 9:5–6: "And surely your blood of your lives will I require; at the hand of every beast will I require it, and at the hand of man; at the hand of every man's brother will I require the life of man. Whoso sheddeth man's blood, by man shall his blood be shed: for in the image of God made he man."

As a preacher and a pastor, I have had drunks call me in the middle of the night. One night, this drunk called me about 2:00 am and wanted me to come and talk to him. I could tell he was drunk, so I told him to go back to bed, and I'd come in the morning when he had sobered up. Then he said, "It is now or never. It's now or never." I said, "Ok, I'll be there as quickly as I can get there." When I got there, he had been drinking even more. His speech was more slurred than it was on the phone, and he finally fell over on the bed, passed out, so I left. He never called me when he was sober, always when he had been drinking. Proverbs 20:1 says, "Wine is a mocker, strong drink is raging: and whosoever is deceived thereby is not wise." Proverbs 23:29–32 says, "Who hath woe? Who hath sorrow? Who hath contentions? Who hath babbling? Who hath wounds without cause? Who hath redness of eyes? They that tarry long at the wine; they that go to seek mixed wine. Look not thou upon the wine when it is red, when it giveth his colour in the cup, when it moveth itself aright. At the last it hiteth like a serpent, and stingeth like an adder."

Hospital Visitation

I have spent a lot of time in the hospitals, especially when there are surgeries. I always try to get there in time to have prayer before they are taken to surgery. There have been times that they have already gone back. I have caught up with them in the holding area. If that is possible, sometimes it is not possible because they will not let you in.

I always ask what time their surgery is scheduled. There is a difference between the time they are to check in and the time their surgery is scheduled, which is usually a two-hour difference. There have been times that they told me their surgery was scheduled for the time they were to check in. It takes a while to get them ready for surgery, and they ask a lot of personal questions that they would not want their pastor to hear.

When I first began to pastor, I would stay from before surgery until they came out of the recovery room. Recovery usually takes one to one-half hours. I was spending too much time in the hospitals. Now when surgery is over, I usually tell the family I will be praying for the patient and leave.

I have had some bad experiences while waiting on surgeries. One lady was to have surgery. We waited for about two hours for them to come and get her. Finally, we found out the surgery had been canceled until the next day.

Another occasion was at the Chapel Hill Hospital. My brother Everett had a very serious surgery. The doctor said it would be a six-hour surgery. We waited six hours with no word that surgery was over. So, I went to find out when the surgery would be over. He was supposed to go to intensive care after surgery, so I went to the intensive care unit. They said he was not here. I asked them to find out when he would be coming into their unit. After they called, they said they were taking him back to his regular room right then. The surgery had been finished in four hours, and we had not heard a word about how the surgery went or that it was finished. His wife Lois sure got on that doctor's case because he did not come and talk to her about the surgery when it was over.

One of the longest surgeries that I ever sat through was Carolyn's sister Linda's husband, Donald "Bo" Bullock. He had cancer of the jaw and tongue brought about by dipping Copenhagen dipping tobacco. They took his jawbone out and sliced his tongue a piece at a time and sent it to the lab each time until no cancer was detected. They did not want to take his whole tongue out. It took fourteen hours.

On the other hand, I have enjoyed the fellowship with families while waiting on surgeries to be finished. It is a time of comfort for most families to have their pastor present. I found out how true that was when Sherry and Carolyn had surgery; our members and friends would show up. It is a blessing to have their company.

Radio Ministry

I was at Camp Zion in Myrtle, Mississippi, which I attended many times. Dr. Percy Ray was the founder. It was there in January 1971 that God spoke to me about starting a radio ministry on WWNC Radio 570 AM in Asheville, North Carolina. Brother Jim Whitted worked at the Citizen Times Building, and WWNC was on the second floor. On that day, when I went to see about buying time for a thirty-minute program, I told Jim I was going to get on WWNC radio. He said, "Good luck," for he didn't think I would get it. I told him go with me because he was familiar with the building. So, he went with me. When I talked to the manager, he said I have thirty minutes open from 7:30–8:00 am on Sundays. I started on February 14, 1971. Thus, my radio ministry began and has continued for fifty-one years so far. Jim began with me from the first broadcast as my announcer. I do not remember how long he continued with me, but later he went to Tabernacle Bible Instute . He was a very special friend. I stayed on WWNC for twenty-three years, and when I moved to Zion Baptist in Gastonia, North Carolina. It was then that I dropped WWNC. I received more mail and support on that station than any other station (except Radio Paradise) that I've been on since. WWNC was the number-one station of the nation for several years. Rev. James Whitted passed away on October 21, 2017, at the age of eighty-two.

Dr. James "Jim" Whitted

When I went to Zion Hill in Marion, North Carolina. I also had a program on the big WAGI, 105.3 FM out of Gaffney, South Carolina. I was on that station until it was sold and became a Spanish-speaking station in April 2007. I was on WCKY AM, broadcasting out of Cincinnati, Ohio. It was a 50,000-watt station. It reached all up and down the Eastern seaboard. It had a great outreach.

When I moved to Gastonia, North Carolina, I went on WLTC in Gastonia, also on WCGC in Belmont, North Carolina. I was on the latter until it became a Catholic station in January 2019. In February 2019, I went on WAVO out of Rock Hill, South Carolina, until May 30, 2020, because it was sold not long after I went on it. I was also on Radio Paradise on the island of St. Kitts, in the Leeward Islands. I received a lot of letters from those people in the island, but it was more of a mission work. Those people were poor and could not send much money, but they sent letters. Further, I was on WAAK Radio out of Dallas, North Carolina, WWNL out of Pittsburgh, Pennsylvania. We have to get the seed out of the barn to the world. Thank God for the open door of radio and TV.

Through the radio and TV ministry, I have gained a lot of supporters and friends.

Mrs. Ruby Wright from Grover, North Carolina, saw the TV program, "The Bible Hour," and became a supporter. Ruby and her son, Brother James Wright Jr., also from Grover, were faithful supporters of the TV program from January 2011. Ruby passed away on January 3, 2018, and I had the privilege of officiating at her funeral. Brother James Jr. and his sister Betty McKee and husband Gene from Shelby, North Carolina, began attending Zion following Mrs. Ruby's death, and all three joined Zion on November 4, 2018. Brother James Wright died

September 14, 2021 at the age of sixty-nine years old.

Ruby Wright

Brother Ronnie McDonald and his wife, Pat, drove from Kannapolis, North Carolina, to be with us so many times. I called him "Ronald McDonald" for a good while. One day, he said, "My name is Ronnie McDonald and not Ronald."

Left to right: Pat (Ronnie's wife), Mike (his son), me, Ronnie McDonald

Also, Brother Willie Lane and wife Judy saw our TV program and came to visit. He would brighten our services with his singing. He and his wife, Judy, drove all the way from Rockwell, North Carolina, which is about a one-hundred-twenty-mile round trip. They were a great blessing.

There was Brother Don Carras, who also saw the TV program, called in, and received an invitation to come and visit. The Sunday that he came to Zion, when he saw the church, he drove past and went down to the intersection and turned around. He thought the church was too small for him to come inside. He was used to going to a big church in Charlotte, North Carolina, Forest Hill Church, which seated 6500 people. But the Lord put in his heart to stop and go inside. He was so blessed that he joined the church on June 9, 2013, and brought several of his friends, which have become my friends also. Brother Bubba Pearsall and his friend Cynthia Drum have brightened our lives when they get to come. Don had a great sense of humor. When he brought some of his friends to church, I would say, "Who are your friends?" He would say, "I picked them up on the side of the road hitchhiking." He was only kidding. Brother Don wasn't with us very long, for cancer took him away on September 18, 2014. He was only sixty-one years old. It was a privilege to speak at Brother Don's funeral at Forest Hill Church in Charlotte.

Don Carras

Another was a man who was brought to Zion who was faithful in watching the TV program. He was a retired airplane pilot and nearly blind. He had to watch the TV with binoculars. He wanted to come and see us in person before he died. It was a great honor to meet the Christian brother who would go to all that trouble to watch the program with binoculars. Not many would go to that much trouble, especially a religious program. He was from Glen Alpine, North Carolina, in Burke County.

Another faithful supporter of the Bible Hour tv program is the Brown family of Rockingham, NC. They have been so faithful every month with their monthly gifts. Thank God for faithful friends like them.

Radio & TV stations I have been on

WPTL	Canton, NC	920 AM	8/31/69–12/28/69
WWNC	Asheville, NC	570 AM	2/14/71-
WAGI	Gaffney, SC	105.3 FM	10/13/74–4/—/07
WBRM	Marion, NC	1250 AM	3/1/81
Radio Paradise,	St. Kitts,	825 AM	8/15/89
WXBG	Burgaw, NC		6/11/89–5/13/90
WXMB	Surfside Beach, SC	101.5 FM	6/11/89–6/10/90
WXCH	Charleston, SC		6/11/89–6/10/90
WCKY	Cincinnati, OH	1530 AM	9/5/93–11/21/93
WKYH	Cincinnati, OH	600 AM	
WLTC	Gastonia, NC	1270 AM	
WDEX	Monroe, NC	1430 AM	
WRKB	Kannapolis, NC	1460 AM	
WRNA	Concord, NC & Chester, SC	1140 AM	
WKMT	Kings Mtn, NC	1220 AM	6/21/98
WCGC	Belmont, NC	1270 AM	11/2010–1/2019
WAVO	Rock Hill, SC	1150 AM	12/2/19–5/30/20
WAAR	Dallas, NC	1260 AM	8/20/04
WWNL	Pittsburgh, PA	1080 AM	6/02/07–11/23/08
WCRU	Winston Salem & Dallas, NC	960 AM 105.7 FM	8/2/20–present

WHKY-TV	Hickory, NC	Ch. 14	3/6/79–6/5/79 First time (while at Zion Hill)
WHKY-TV	Hickory, NC	Ch. 14	9/18/02–present
ACCN-TV (While at Zion Hill)	Asheville, NC	Ch. 2	
Time Warner Cable		Ch. 58, 9, 14, 18	
Charter	Hickory, NC	Ch. 7, 10	

Me editing the TV program

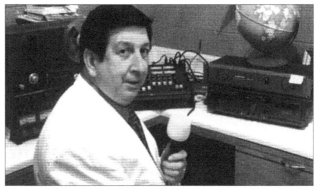

Me recording the radio program

Tribute to Carolyn

Carolyn was fifteen years old when this photo was taken.

I would like to give a tribute to my wonderful wife, Carolyn. She has been by my side since 1957. She has been there through the good times and the tough times. She has been such a special lady. She gave birth to three wonderful children who love God. She has been a great wife, who washes and irons my clothes so I always look neat. Further, she is a tremendous cook. I tell her that she is a "mountain cook" who knows how to make a fabulous meal. She is a lady with a big heart. She is like her Grandmother Austin, who gave everyone in the family a gift at Christmas time. It might have just been socks or a box of handkerchiefs, but she gave everyone something. When I married Carolyn, Grandmother Austin put my name on her list. She lived on a very limited income, but she was able to give.

Carolyn keeps up with all the family's birthdays, the kids' birthdays, and the grandkids' birthdays, still further, the great grandkids' birthdays. She always sends them all a birthday present. Even close friends—she keeps up with their birthday and sends a happy birthday card or either gives them a call to wish them a happy birthday.

Carolyn has spent a lot of time sitting with the sick in her lifetime, not only with my family and her family but also with a host of friends and church members. Among them was my mother and her mother. Carolyn's mother, Vervena House, was diagnosed with pancreatic cancer in November 1989. She passed away on February 2, 1990. Carolyn and her two sisters, Sandy and Vicky, would take a night about sitting up with their mother. We were living in Marion, North Carolina, at that time. Carolyn drove up to Candler in the evening time, spent the night, and would leave out at 4:00

am to drive back to Marion, get ready for work, and drive to Morganton to work at Hanes, which was thirty miles from our house. She had to be at work at 7:00 am. She sat up every third night for a year. Further, she sat with her daddy, my Aunt Zora, and many others. To name them all would be a long list of people.

Carolyn is a tremendous pastor's wife. She is friendly with everybody. She always tries to shake hands with the visitors who come to church. Further, she is always laughing and upbeat. One man made a statement that when she came in the door of the church, he could hear her talking and laughing. Pastor Billy Bryant told her, "When you walk into a room, it is like a ray of sunshine walked in." Still further, she has a lot of wisdom and discernment, which is a great blessing to me as a pastor. Again, she is a woman of prayer who can get a hold of God and ring the prayer bells of heaven.

Carolyn is like a mother to the church congregation. Everyone looks to her for guidance, an ear to listen, and a shoulder to cry on. Carolyn knows just the right thing to say to lift your spirits and knows when to give you a much-needed hug. Many people look to her for prayer, not just because she's the preacher's wife but also because she is a tremendous prayer warrior and has a lot of compassion. But you better not say anything bad about the preacher. She's like Scott Fish about that. She will fight you over her kids and her husband.

At Christmas time, Carolyn always cooks, not only for our family that will be coming but also a host of others who are invited to come by for a Christmas meal. George and Marsha Steel eat with us on Christmas Day. That is just a tradition that has been going on for a long time.

Carolyn had three sisters, Sandy, Linda, and Vickie, and one brother, Billy House, who passed away on April 17, 2010, at the age of sixty-six. Billy had a big heart and was a very loving person. He had four boys, Jerry, Richard, James, and Bobby. The first three have passed away, along with Billy's wife, Ann. Bobby is the only one still alive. He lives in Hendersonville, North Carolina. Every year on Family Day at Zion Baptist Church, Bobby brings his motorcycle club. They really enjoy the ride from Hendersonville to Gastonia. We enjoy seeing the convoy drive into our parking lot. Still further, they bring excitement in our service. It is a blessing to Bobby and his family, along with all his motorcycle friends and the church family. Carolyn's sister Vickie passed away on December 12, 2021, at the age of sixty-two.

Carolyn with her brother Billy
The last time Carolyn saw Billy alive
in Daytona, Florida

Me, Billy House, & wife Ann
This was the last time I saw Billy alive.

Carolyn, Billy House, Sandy Whitaker, Linda Gillard,
Vicky Collura, Carolyn's brother and sisters

Carolyn was the only girl I ever dated. There were girls in our community who I liked and also at school, but Carolyn was the only girl I ever dated.

Carolyn House in 1956

**Made in front of
the Dead Sea Scrolls Cave**

Easter Sunday

**Hot air balloon ride–balloon
operator in green shirt,
Patty–Bill Erwin's sister, Bill Erwin,
Carolyn, unknown woman in back**

Quotes

Calf rope, Lord (Lord, I surrender)

Stick up your ears like an old mule (pay attention).

Finer than snuff and not half as dusty (that is Fine)

When the Big Preacher comes, the little preacher sits down.

Ride the waves (if they are up, you ride them up, and if they are down, you ride them down. Whatever life's circumstances are that you can't change, either endure them or enjoy them).

Grandma was slow, but she was old (speed up).

Buckle your seat belt and let's go.

This is guaranteed, or your money back isn't it (I like to say this to clerks and hear what they reply).

We are on the little end of something big.

I was going through a cafeteria line, and I said, "Give me some banana pudding. I think there is going to be banana pudding in heaven, don't you?" She replied sternly, "I don't think so."

People ask me, "How are you," and I say, "Up one hill and down another." That is the way life is.

My Experience with Cars

I have had quite a few cars in my lifetime. Some were good and some not so good.

The first car I owned was a 1942 Ford that I bought from my brother James Alvin. Later, I traded for a 1951 Chevrolet Fleet Back. It had a big duck ornament on the hood. I thought it was something. That is the car that I courted Carolyn in and also took our honeymoon to Florida in. Then I traded for a 1952 Ford. I broke the driver's side window twice because the door was so hard to shut. I traded that car for a 1960 Chevrolet Impala. I ordered it with special features, a hard top, tinted glass, and a straight shift with overdrive. Would that Impala run! I could do seventy miles per hour in second gear. I have had new Volkswagens and Hondas. The best cars of all are Hondas. They have given me many miles of maintenance-free driving. I had a 1989 Honda Civic of which I put 233,000 miles on it before I wrecked it on Neal Hawkins Rd. A lady stopped in front of me, and I couldn't stop in time. I got forty miles to the gallon of gas even with that many miles on it. Still further, I put 200,000 miles on it before I changed the plugs. The gap on the plugs was ninety thousandths. And most cars would not even start with plug gaps that large. The Lord has blessed my cars.

Here is a little story that people will not believe this day and time, but it is true. I went to Orlando, Florida, and back for ten dollars' worth of gas. I had a 1971 Volkswagen, which got thirty miles to the gallon. There was a gas war going on at that time, and gas was nineteen cents to twenty cents per gallon. You can figure it. Ten dollars would have bought fifty gallons of gas. Fifty gallons times thirty miles per gallon would be 1500 miles. Don't you wish you could go back to the good old days of gas prices like in those days?

My Experience with Snakes

I had two encounters with copperhead snakes. One, I had bailed some hay and staked it under the barn shed. Papaw Medford and I were up at the barn checking on the hay. I pulled a bail off the stake to see if it was heating up. Low and behold, there lay a big copperhead. I said, "Papaw, watch the snake, and I will run and get the gun." When I returned with the gun, Papaw was still looking for the snake. That is how well they blend in with their surroundings. I didn't even aim. I just pointed the gun and shot. The snake crawled between the hay and the barn. I had shot two or three times more, and he crawled out of sight. I thought, *There is no way that I missed him.* We pulled out several bales of hay, and when we found him, I had blown him all to pieces.

A second time, Carolyn and I went to eat with a Rev. Charles Worley and his wife on South Turkey in Leicester, North Carolina. This Charles Worley was a member of my church, Good News Baptist, not the Charles Worley I baptized in the Jordan River. After dinner, he said, "Let's walk over to the barn, and I'll show you Daddy's barn and his farm." When we got there and started around the corn crib, all of a sudden, he said, "Stop, don't move. There's a copperhead." I said, "Where?" I kept looking, but I didn't see it. He grabbed a big pole and came down on the snake, and then I saw it. It was only four or five feet away from me. It certainly could have bit me. I thank God it didn't.

Dreaming about Snakes

Some people will laugh at what I am about to tell you or simply say it is only a fantasy. I will not watch snakes on TV. I don't want to dream about them. If I dream about snakes, it is the Lord showing me some trouble that is coming.

I have had several different dreams about snakes, and it always ends in some kind of trouble. One night, I dreamed I was down in a field next to a big brush pile, and one of my members was walking up. I hollered, "Watch out, there is a snake in the brush." About that time, the snake bit him. A short time after that, he got mad and left the church.

I do not like to dream about snakes, but when I do, I know the Lord is warning me about trouble to come.

Sermon Flops

My first Mother's Day sermon was a disaster. I preached on "Seven Different Types of Women." I have never lived that sermon down!

On another occasion, I was asked to preach at Happy Valley Baptist Church in West Asheville, North Carolina. Many of the women Carolyn worked with went to that church. I preached on "Ruth's Choice," out of the book of Ruth. Carolyn said it was the worst sermon I had ever preached. She wanted me to do so good since many of the women she worked with were there that night. Sometimes we fall on our faces. But I'm glad to know what the Bible says in Isaiah 55:11, "So shall my word be that goeth forth out of my mouth, it shall not return unto me void, but it shall accomplish that which I please, and it shall prosper in the things whereunto I sent it." Sometimes the sermons we think are so bad, God uses them to touch someone's life.

Sermon Preparation: Practical Things

My method of preaching as a pastor has been that I usually preach Evangelistic sermons on Sunday morning. On Sunday night, I preach through the New Testament and then on Wednesday night, I preach through the Old Testament. Paul said in 2 Timothy 4:2, "Preach the Word." Hosea 4:6 says, "My people are destroyed for lack of knowledge." I certainly don't want my people (members) to be lacking in the knowledge of the Lord. Spurgeon said, "Variety boys, Variety boys." (Lectures to My Students). Still further, Jesus told Peter in John 21:16 to "feed my sheep." That is what I want to do. I have had several people tell me that they have learned more under my preaching than any church that they have been in. That does not give me the "big head," but it humbles me. Thank God that the Lord can use me in a very small way.

Different preachers do different ways in their sermon preparation. Some type out their sermons. Others may use a tablet. Some use composition books, and still others may preach from the hip. Every preacher uses the method that works best for him.

I use 4 ½ x 7 ½ sheets of paper that fit in my Scofield Bible. I have a printing company to cut my paper. This works for me because if I want to add pages to my sermons that are already prepared, it is easy to insert another page. This I do in so many of my sermons. All I have to do is, for example, title my pages 1, next 1b, next 1c, and 2, 2a, 2b, and so on, depending on whether I need to insert an additional thought.

"A merry heart doeth good like a medicine."
Proverbs 17:22

Carolyn's Birthday—Hawaiian Luau

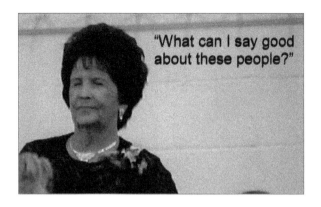

My birthday party–A "50s sock hop"

Valentine's Dinner

At Jr. & Susie Ogle's wedding
vow renewal

Carolyn & me, July 4, 2021
Zion Baptist

Carolyn, Linda, & Rev. Tom Walker & myself
Zion Hill homecoming – August 22, 2021

Carolyn's "heaven sent" birthday party

Through the years

Zion Hill parsonage drive

Zion Baptist parsonage drive

Zion Baptist stage area

The Lord is My:

1. Beloved (Song of Sol. 5:16)
2. Buckler (Ps. 18:2)
3. Creator (Ps. 119:73)
4. Defense (Ps. 7:10, 59:9, 16–17, 62:2)
5. Deliverer (2 Sam. 22:2; Ps. 6:4, 7:1, 18:1–2, 40:17)
6. Fortress (2 Sam. 22:2, 31:3, 91:2)
7. Glory (Ps. 3:3)
8. God (Ps. 18:2, 5:2, 18:1–2, 31:14, 35:23, 40:17, 42:6, 42:11, 43:4, 43:5, 71:4, 71:22, 84:3, 84:10, 86:2, 86:12, 91:2)
9. God of my salvation (Ps. 88:1)
10. Goodness (Ps. 144:2)
11. Healer (Ps. 6:2)
12. Health of my countenance (Ps. 42:11, 43:5)
13. Help (Ps. 27:9, 33:20, 40:17, 71:12)
14. Helper (Heb. 13:6; Ps. 54:4)
15. Hiding place (Ps. 32:7, 119:114)
16. Hope (Ps. 38:15, 71:5)
17. Horn of my salvation (Ps. 18:2)
18. Joy (exceeding) (Ps. 43:4)
19. Judge (Ps. 7:8)
20. Justification (Romans 4:25)
21. Keeper (Ps. 121:5)
22. King (Ps. 5:2, 44:4, 72:12, 84:3)
23. Lifter up of mine head (Ps. 3:3)
24. Light (Ps. 27:1)
25. Lord (Ps. 16:1, 35:23)
26. Mercy (Ps. 59:17)
27. Portion (Lam. 3:24)
28. Portion forever (Ps. 73:26)
29. Power (2 Sam. 22:33)
30. Redeemer (Ps. 19:14)
31. Redemption (1 Cor. 1:30)
32. Refuge (2 Sam. 22:3; Ps. 9:9, 59:16, 91:2, 91:9)
33. Rightousness (1 Cor. 1:30; Ps. 4:1)
34. Rock (2 Sam. 22:3; Ps. 18:1–2, 31:3, 42:9, 62:2, 92:15)
35. Salvation (Ps. 18:46, 38:22, 62:2)
36. Sanctification (1 Cor. 1:30)
37. Saviour (2 Sam. 22:3)
38. Shield (2 Sam. 22:3; Ps. 3:3, 28:7, 33:20)
39. Song (Ps. 118:14)
40. Stay (Ps. 18:18)
41. Strength (2 Sam. 22:33; Ps. 18:1–2, 28:7, 31:4, 43:2, 59:17)

42. Strong refuge (Ps. 71:7)
43. Tower (high) (2 Sam. 22:3; Ps. 18:2)
44. Trust (Ps. 71:5)
45. Wisdom (1 Cor. 1:30)

THE LORD IS MY SHEPHERD
PSALM 23:1

HE IS MY ALL IN ALL

"I will sing unto the Lord as long as I live:
I will sing praise to my God while I have my being." Psalm 104:33

"Because he hath inclined his ear unto me,
therefore will I call upon him as long as I live." Psalm 116:2

"While I live will I praise the Lord:
I will sing praises unto my God while I have any being." Psalm 146:2

"My righteousness I hold fast, and will not let it go: My
heart shall not reproach me so long as live." Job 27:6

"Be thou in the fear of the Lord all the day long." Prov. 23:17

A Sermon Outline on Things of Great Worth

I. A person worth knowing (that Person is Jesus Christ)
    1. Savior of the world (John 4:42)
    2. Author and finisher of our faith (Heb. 12:2)
    3. Alpha and Omega (Rev. 1:8)
    4. King of kings and Lord of lords (Rev. 17:14, 19:16)
    5. Our Shepherd (John 10:11; Ps. 23:1)
    6. Read Philippians 3:8–14.

II. A position worth filling (being a)
    1. Saint (Rom. 1:7)
    2. Son of God (1 John 3:1)
    3. Servant (Rom. 6:18, 22; Rev. 1:1)
    4. Soldier (2 Tim. 2:3–4)
    5. Sheep (Ps. 100:3; John 10:3)

III. A truth worth knowing
    1. That you are saved
    2. That you have eternal life (1 John 3:14, 5:13)
    3. Eternal life vs. eternal death

IV. A joy worth having
    1. The joy of the Lord (Matt. 25:21, 23)
    2. The joy of salvation (Ps. 51:12)
    3. The joy of the Lord is your strength (Neh. 8:10)
    4. The joy of faith (Phil. 1:25)
    5. The joy of the Holy Ghost (1 Thess. 1:6)

V. A place worth (being) attending.
    1. In the house of the Lord (Ps. 23:6, 92:13)
    2. On the Lord's day
    3. Psalm 27:4: "that I may dwell in the house of the Lord all the days of my life."
    4. Psalm 84:4: "Blessed are they that dwell in thy house."
    5. Psalm 84:10: "For a day in the courts is better than a thousand (days)."

VI. A book worth reading (the Word of God)
    1. The Bible (Luke 4:4: "man shall not live by bread alone, but by every word of God.")
    2. The book of all books (Prov. 30:5: "Every word of God is pure.")
    3. The Bible is:
        1. Inspired
        2. Inerrant
        3. Infallible
        4. Indestructible Word of God (Ps. 12:6–7, 19:7–11; Isa. 40:8)

4. Read the Bible
    1. To know the truth (Ps. 33:4, 119:43)
    2. To be saved
    3. To be wise
    4. To be holy

VII. A gift worth giving
    1. Your talent
    2. Your time (God asks for one day out of seven).
    3. Your tithe (one-tenth of your income belongs to the Lord. The tithe is the Lord's).

VIII. A service worth rendering (soul-winning)
    1. Proverbs 11:30: "He that winneth souls is wise."
    2. Daniel 12:3: "and they that be wise shall shine as the brightness of the firmament and they that turn many to righteousness as the stars forever and ever."
    3. Matthew 5:14–15 (let your light so shine)
    4. John 4:34–37 (v. 35): "lift up your eyes, and look on the fields; for they are white already to harvest."

IX. A day worth remembering
    1. The Lord's day (Rev. 1:10; Exod. 20:8)
    2. A Sabbath of rest
    For the Jews, the Sabbath is a day of:
        1. Resting;
        2. Eating;
        3. Praying;
        4. Sleeping;
        5. Reading;
        6. Thinking;
        7. Studying;
        8. Talking;
        9. Listening;
        10. Meditating;
        11. Visiting the sick;
        12. Laughing;
        13. Singing;
        14. Welcoming guests;
        15. Teaching children; and
        16. A day of blessings.
        We need the Lord's day:
            1. Physically;
            2. Mentally;
            3. Socially;
            4. Domestically; and

     5.   Spiritually.

X.   Thoughts worth thinking (Phil. 4:8)
"Whatsoever is:
1. True;
2. Honest;
3. Just;
4. Pure;
5. Lovely; and
6. Good report.
   If there be any:
7. Virtue; and
8. Praise;
   Think on these things.

XI. A foundation worth building on (build your life on Christ)
1. 1 Corinthians 3:11–15 (v. 11): "For other foundation can no man lay than that is laid, which is Jesus Christ."
2. Matthew 7:24–27 (v. 24) "whosoever heareth these sayings of mine, and doeth them, I will liken him unto a wise man, which built his house upon a rock."

XII. A crown worth winning
1. Crown of Life Revelation 2:5, James 1:12
2. Incorruptible Crown l Corinthians 9:25
3. Crown of Rejoicing l Thessalonians 2:9
4. Crown of Righteousness l Timothy 4:8
5. Crown of Glory l Peter 5:4

XIII.A reward worth receiving
1. What he will say: Matthew 25:23
   (1) "Well done thy good and faithful servant
   (2) Thou hast been faithful over a few things.
   (3) I will make the ruler over many things."
   (4) Enter into the joy of thy Lord."
2. What he will give; Revelation 22:12 (rewards are earned); Romans 6:23 (eternal life is a gift)

XIV. A place worth going (heaven, the New Jerusalem)
1. The land of all lands
2. The home of all homes
3. The place of places
4. The dwelling place of God the Father, God the Son, and God the Holy Spirit
5. The land of freedom and rest
6. The land of "No mores" (Rev. 21–22)
1. Crying

2. Sighing
3. Sorrow
4. Sickness
5. Pain
6. Dying
7. Curse
8. Sin
9. Temptation
10. Devil

XV. A soul worth saving (your own soul)
   1. Possession of the soul (Mark 8:36–37)
   2. Image of the soul (made in the image of God)
   3. Capacity of the soul (forever growing and learning through eternity)
   4. Value of the soul (worth more than the whole world).
   5. The eternity of the soul (your soul will live on through the ages of ages, either in heaven or hell; you can buy a lot of things with money, but you can't buy a home in heaven)

XVI. A prayer worth praying (a sinner's prayer)
   1. Like the publican (God be merciful to me, a sinner). Luke 18:13
   2. Like the thief on the cross (Lord, remember me when thou comest into thy kingdom). Luke 23:42
   3. Like the prodigal son (Father, I have sinned against heaven and in thy sight). Luke 15:21
      1. The prayer of confession
      2. The prayer of repentance
      3. The prayer of surrender
      4. The prayer of faith (Lord, I believe)

These three songs I love to hear Sherry sing:

Amazing Grace (My Chains Are Gone)
By
By Chris Tomlin

Amazing Grace, how sweet the sound
That saved a wretch like me
I once was lost, but now I'm found
Was blind but now I see

'Twas grace that taught my heart to fear
And grace my fears relieved
How precious did that grace appear
The hour I first believed

My chains are gone
I've been set free
My God, my Savior has ransomed me
And like a flood
His mercy reigns
Unending love
Amazing Grace

The Lord has promised good to me
His word my hopes secures
He will my shield and portion be
As long as life endures

My chains are gone
I've been set free
My God, my Savior has ransomed me
And like a flood
His mercy reigns
Unending love
Amazing Grace

The earth shall soon dissolve like snow
The sun forebear to shine
But God, who called me here below
Will be forever mine
Will be forever mine
You are forever mine

O What a Savior Is Mine
By
Betty jean Robinson

Bethlehem Calvary,
All of it tell

O what a savior is mine,
Mountain and plains
With His praises shall swell
O what a savior is mine

O what a savior, O what a savior
O what a savior is mine
Unto the uttermost
Wonderful glorious
O what a savior is mine

There on the cross
Where He died for my sins
O what a savior is mine
Giving His life
A poor wanderer to men
O what a savior is mine

O what a savior, O what a savior
O what a savior is mine
Unto the uttermost
Wonderful, glorious
O what a savior is mine

Lifting my burdens
Relieving my cares
O what a savior is mine
Giving me courage
To do and to dare
O what a savior is mine

O what a savior, O what a savior
O what a savior is mine
Unto the uttermost
Wonderful, glorious
O what a savior is mine

Sweet Jesus
By
Cyril McLellan

Sweet Jesus, Sweet Jesus
What a wonder you are
You're brighter than the morning star
You're fairer, much fairer
Than the lilies that bloom by the wayside
Precious, more precious than gold

He cleansed the spotted leopard
He opened blinded eyes
He walked on troubled waters
He astounded passers by
He forgave the sinful woman and
He raised Lazarus from the dead and
He broke bread from one small loaf
And he ten thousand fed

Sweet Jesus, Sweet Jesus
What a wonder you are
You're brighter than the morning star
You're fairer, much fairer
Than the lilies that bloom by the wayside
Precious, more precious than gold

He's the oak and I'm the ivy
He's the potter and I'm the clay
He's the oil and I'm the vessel
I'm the traveler and He's the way
I'm the flower and He's the fragrance
I'm the lamp and He's the flame
He's the words I sing to music and
I'm the bride that claims His name

Sweet Jesus, Sweet Jesus
What a wonder you are
You're brighter than the morning star
You're fairer, much fairer
Than the lilies that bloom by the wayside
Precious, more precious than gold

Old Time Preacher Man

(Written by Mary Ball)

Leo is an old-time preacher man
He preached the Word of God throughout the land
He preached so plain a child could understand
Oh, Leo was an old-time preacher man.

In them there hills little Leo went to school
A riding on his one short-legged mule
He never was ashamed to take a stand
Cause he walked just like his mule, this preacher man

Little Leo had a real tough row to hoe
But taters, maters and biscuits made him grow
With a Bible and a plow line in each hand
He vowed that he would be a preacher man

When Leo went to see his only girl
She was the prettiest gal in all the world
When she kissed him his hair began to curl
She gave little Leo's hair a whirl

Now Leo has become a preacher man
We think he is the best one in the land
When he cranks-up he preaches to beat the band
Oh, Leo is an old-time preacher man

Leo is our old-time preacher man
We know he is the best one in the land
He makes the way to heaven seem so sweet
And preaches hell so hot that you can feel the heat

Oh, Leo is an old-time preacher man.

So Much to Thank Him For
By
Marvin Morrow

When I look around and see, the good things He does for me
I know I'm unworthy of them all, but His blessings He freely gives
I owe my life to Him I've got so much to thank Him for.

I've got so much to thank Him for; so much to praise Him for.
You see how He's been so good to me.
And when I think of what He's done
And where He brought me from, I've got so much to thank Him for.

And sometimes while on this way, I kneel, I stop and say,
Thank You for all You've done for me.
And one day I'll reach heaven's shore, oh please just let me kneel once more
I've got so much to thank Him for.

I've got so much to thank Him for; so much to praise Him for.
You see how He's been so good to me.
And when I think of what He's done
And where He brought me from, I've got so much to thank Him for.

When I think of what He's done and where He's brought me from,
I've got so much to thank Him for!

Thank You Lord!

The ABC of Salvation

I. Acknowledge
1. That Jesus Christ is the Savior of the world
2. That you are a sinner; Jesus came to seek and to save them which was lost.

II. Believe in the Lord Jesus Christ
1. John 3:15 – "That whosoever believeth in him should not perish, but have eternal life."
2. John 3:16 – "For God so loved the world, that he gave his only begotten Son, that whosoever believeth in him should not perish, but have everlasting life."
3. Romans 10:10 – "For with the heart man believeth unto righteousness; and with the mouth confession is made unto salvation."
4. Romans 10:11 – "For the scripture saith, whosoever believeth on him shall not be ashamed."

III. Call upon the Lord
Romans 10:13 – "For whosoever shall call upon the name of the Lord shall be saved."

IV. Confess Christ as your Savior
Romans 10:10 – "For with the heart man believeth unto righteousness; and with the mouth confession is made unto salvation."

Examples:
1. Simon Peter said to Christ, "Thou art the Christ the son of the living God" (Matt. 16:16).
2. Martha, "She saith unto him, Yea, Lord: I believe that thou art the Christ, the Son of God, which should come into the world" (John 11:27).
3. Ethiopian eunuch said, "I believe that Jesus Christ is the Son of God" (Acts 8:37).

V. Repent – Be sorry enough for your sins enough to turn from them and turn to Christ.
1   Mark 6:12 – "And they went out, and preached that men should repent."
2   Luke 13:3 – "I tell you, Nay: but except ye repent, ye shall all likewise perish."
3. Acts 3:19 – "Repent ye therefore, and be converted, that your sins may be blotted out, when the times of refreshing shall come from the presence of the Lord."
4   Acts 17:30 – "And the times of this ignorance God winked at; but now commandeth all men everywhere torepent
5. Acts 26:20 – (Paul) "But shewed first unto them of Damascus, and at Jerusalem, and throughout all the coasts of Judea, and then to the Gentiles, that they should repent and turn to God, and do works meet for repentance."

6. 2 Peter 3:9 – "The Lord is not slack concerning his promise, as some men count slackness; but is longsuffering to us-ward, not willing that any should perish, but that all should come to repentance."
7. Luke 5:32 – "I came not to call the righteous, but sinners to repentance."
8. John 8:24 – "I said therefore unto you, that ye shall die in your sins: for if ye believe not that I am he, ye shall die in your sins."

VI. Follow Christ
   1. Matthew 16:24 – "Then said Jesus unto his disciples, if any man will come after me, let him deny himself, and
   Tahe up his cross and follow Me."
   2. John 10:27 – "My sheep hear My voice, and I know them, and they follow Me."
   3. Don't stop here. Go on to:
   4. Be Baptized
      A. Scripturally
         (1) Not sprinkled
         (2) But by emersion
      B. Jesus was baptized
      C. Jesus commanded baptism (Matt. 28:18–20)
   5. Join a Bible-believing church, a Bible-preaching church.
   6. Read the Bible every day (the King James Version)
   7. Be a Witness for Jesus
   8. Let your light shine.
   9. Tell others about Jesus Christ, the Savior of the world.

I can't close without giving you an invitation to come to Christ.

"Come now, and let us reason together, saith the Lord: though your sins be as scarlet, they shall be white as snow, though they be red like crimson, they shall be as wool." Isaiah 1:18. "Come unto Me, all ye that labour and are heavy laden, and I will give you rest." Matthew 11:28.

Here is God's last invitation in the Bible:

Revelation 22:17

"And the Spirit and the Bride say, come.
And let him that heareth say, come.
And let him that is athirst, come.
and whosoever will, let him take the water of life freely."

Call or write to:
Rev. Leo Kuykendall
%Zion Baptist Church
2437 Propst Street
Gastonia, NC 28056

leocarolyn@bellsouth.net

704-867-2550

Lightning Source UK Ltd.
Milton Keynes UK
UKHW050803250123
415867UK00011B/77